DYLAN
a man called alias

RICHARD WILLIAMS

DYLAN

a man called alias

RICHARD WILLIAMS

HENRY HOLT AND COMPANY
New York

Copyright © 1992 by Richard Williams
All rights reserved, including the right to reproduce
this book or portions thereof in any form.
First published in the United States in 1992 by
Henry Holt and Company, Inc., 115 West 18th Street,
New York, New York 10011.
Originally published in Great Britain in 1992 by Bloomsbury
Publishing Ltd.

Library of Congress Cataloging-in-Publication Data

Williams, Richard.
    Bob Dylan: a man called Alias / Richard Williams. — 1st
American ed.
        p.   cm.
    1. Dylan, Bob, 1941–   . 2. Rock Musicians — United States —
Biography.   I. Title   92-14992
    ML420.D98w58   1992   CIP
    782.42162'0092—dc20   MN
    [B]

ISBN 0-8050-2255-4

Henry Holt Books are available at special discounts
for bulk purchases for sales promotions, premiums,
fund-raising, or educational use. Special editions
or book excerpts can also be created to specification.

For details contact: Special Sales Director,
Henry Holt and Company, Inc., 115 West 18th Street,
New York, New York 10011.

First American Edition—1992

Designed by Bradbury and Williams
Picture research by Jenny Speller
Printed in Hong Kong
Recognizing the importance of preserving the written word,
Henry Holt and Company, Inc., by policy, prints all of its
first editions on acid-free paper. ∝

10   9   8   7   6   5   4   3   2   1

PHOTO SOURCES

Jacket
Front, central image: Jan Persson
Front, background images, clockwise from bottom left: David
Wainwright/Relay; Brian Shuel/Redferns; Redferns;
Ken Regan/London Features International;
Aaron Rapoport/Retna Pictures
Back: Jan Persson

Recurring paragraph openers/background images
Introduction: Rex Features
Chapter 1: Hibbing High School, Hibbing, Minnesota
Chapter 2: Jim Marshall
Chapter 3: Jan Persson
Chapter 4: Popperfoto
Chapter 5: Michael Ochs Archives
Chapter 6: Chalkie Davies/Relay
Chapter 7: David Wainwright/Relay
Chapter 8: London Features International

All other photos as credited

For Susanne Vincent

'It's always lonely where I am'
Bob Dylan, 1965

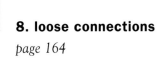

bob dylan's dream

© JAN PERSSON

And still we come at him, flooding his life with our demands. We want him to sing the song we heard in a listening booth in a record shop in the autumn of 1963, pressed up against the girl who'd written on a holiday postcard that she'd heard this singer on French radio called, she thought, 'Bob Dillon', and when she got back home could we try to find his record? Well, we did, and we liked how he and his girlfriend looked on the cover, arm in arm in the street like wise and beautiful children – and tonight we want him to play that song again, and we want him to make it sound just the way it did then. Don't disturb our precious memories, please.

Or maybe we want him to do the song differently, some way that he's never done it before, different from all the ways he's done it over the last thirty years, because he's the guy who reinvents himself, right? Isn't that what he does? Isn't that what we pay him for?

Just imagine what it must be like to live under that kind of assault for thirty years. Imagine, too, knowing that whatever you're doing today,

no matter how trivial or banal it may be, somebody a continent or two away is going to find out about it because he wants to tap the details into his computer, cross-check it against information from his international network of contacts, and file it in the data bank of your life.

If you're Bob Dylan, the world must have seemed a funny place for a long time now. Take 1965. You're twenty-four years old. You've written 'Blowin' in the Wind', 'Masters of War', 'The Lonesome Death of Hattie Carroll', 'The Ballad of Hollis Brown'. You've shared a stage with Martin Luther King. You've made a generation think about war, injustice, oppression. You land at a foreign airport and a reporter says: 'These songs of yours – do you really believe what you're singing about?' Now what are you supposed to say to that?

In a way, it's Bob Dylan's own fault. He started it, when he thought of a name that sounded better than the one he'd been born with and then began making up stories about himself to impress people who otherwise might not have paid much attention to a scrawny storekeeper's son from a little

Minnesota mining town. 'I was playing Bob Dylan' is what he sometimes says to explain a less than fully committed performance, and the price of the myth is the pressure that goes with it. If you create around yourself a character that isn't actually you, then sometimes life is going to get painful.

We bought his myth, all right. It was what we needed. We heard in it the story we wanted to hear, and it led us to invest him with more importance than any other individual of his generation. We needed a symbol, and he let us choose him. But then we told him that he had to be what we wanted him to be: it was part of the contract.

So sometimes we say that he's 'reinvented' himself – as an electric rocker, as a mellow country singer, as a gypsy troubadour. We've taken his changes, and used them to service our own fantasy that life could be lived according to an unbroken series of existential whims. We couldn't quite manage it ourselves, so we allowed him to do it for us.

According to him, though, we'd got it wrong. He was no more 'reinventing' himself than we were. But we'd fallen

in love with the fantasy, we'd bought tickets to it, and we demanded that he live it out. And now we act as if he owes us something.

Nobody's perfect. There have been mediocre records and worse gigs and a terrible movie, and no doubt some regrettable behaviour too. But it's no use trying to make him fit a pattern. Whatever it is that propels him in a certain direction now is the same thing that has prompted all his decisions. It's his spirit, and it made him what he was in the first place. The confusions, the contradictions and the perversity are all part of it, as much an expression of humanity as his masterpieces. And when you sift through the things he's said over the past thirty years, you can't help being struck by the accuracy of his insights into himself.

'I'm only Bob Dylan when I have to be Bob Dylan,' he says. 'Most of the time I'm just myself.' That isn't good enough for us. We want him to be Bob Dylan all the time, and what makes him unique — different from, say, Frank Sinatra or Elvis Presley — is that each of us has a different idea of who Bob Dylan is. This, of course, is a lot of Bob Dylans for him to be. At one extreme, there are said to be more than 500 Bob Dylan fans logged in a police computer file because they've indicated

that they'd like to do him some sort of physical harm. That's 500-plus Bob Dylans, for a start, none of whom has much to do with your idea of Bob Dylan, or mine.

Fans are tricky people. 'I don't think of myself as a fan of anybody,' says the man whose devotion to Hank Williams, Elvis Presley, Little Richard, Jimmy Rodgers, Robert Johnson and Woody Guthrie shaped his own life. 'I'm more of an admirer, so why should I think of anyone as a fan of me?' Since he tries to pay us the compliment of imagining that we can keep our admiration in perspective, we might consider doing the same for him.

He's against interpretation, too, and he can't be blamed for that. He writes a song and he sings it; you listen to it. He doesn't think it's the business of a third party to come along and explain what he meant. Nor does he want us to draw a literal comparison between the events in his songs and those in his life. What an artist does is to take life and turn it into something else. To make the literal interpretation must be to reduce it. So his songs are his songs; they are not his life. And this is Bob Dylan's story; but it is not his life.

1. in the north country

*'A turquoise
guitar, a
motorcycle, and
a girl called
Echo'*

It happened this way. First there was the radio, picking up messages from the twilight zone. Then came the record-player, and the small pile of 45s, each one committed to memory. Then a home-made guitar, or somebody's cast-off, or perhaps an old banjo with half of a set of war-surplus headphones taped under the bridge and plugged into the valve radio to simulate a pick-up and amp. Then a friend with a real guitar, and another with a junk-shop snare drum. And finally, one Saturday afternoon, in a teenage bedroom or an empty garage, the first faltering attempts to mimic those signals coming from some magic place: 'Heartbreak Hotel', perhaps, or 'Rock Island Line'. And the electrifying power — the power that could be felt as the tremulous open E chord led falteringly to the A and the B in the three-chord matrix of rock 'n' roll, and as the backbeat locked in to that pattern — never went away. In those simple elements there was more than just the structure of a song; they contained the outlines, the blueprint, of a new culture

and a new world — something different, anyway, from what your parents had, and what they'd planned for you.

Robert Allen Zimmerman was born on 24 May 1941 in Duluth, northern Minnesota, the son of Abraham and Beatrice Zimmerman. Both parents were descended from East European Jews: Abe's father had owned a shoe factory in the Ukraine, Beatty's grandparents were from Latvia and Lithuania. All of them had fled the rule of

© R. MAIMAN/SYGMA

ROBERT ALLEN ZIMMERMAN: THE CERTIFICATE OF HIS BIRTH AT 9 P.M. ON SATURDAY 24 MAY 1941 IN ST MARY'S HOSPITAL, DULUTH, MINNESOTA.

THE ZIMMERMANS OCCUPIED THE TOP FLOOR OF THIS TWO-FAMILY HOUSE AT 519 THIRD AVENUE EAST, DULUTH.

©JEFF SYME

'THE IRON ORE POURED/AS THE YEARS PASSED THE DOOR/THE DRAG LINES AND THE SHOVELS THEY WAS A-HUMMIN' ': THE HIBBING TACONITE COMPANY OPERATED THIS STRIP MINE ON THE IRON RANGE.

the tsars, in the classic pattern of pre-Great War emigration. Abe, too, had been born in Duluth, where his father worked first as a pedlar and then as a salesman in a shoe shop, slowly building a solid life for a family to which hard work became second nature. Abe, one of half a dozen children, was shining shoes and delivering newspapers from the age of seven, but by the time he married Beatty Stone, in 1934, he had a steady berth at the Duluth office of Standard Oil. They were a cautious couple: seven years of establishing themselves went by before the first of their two children was born.

Abe lost his Standard Oil job in 1945, when the war ended and demand fell. The following year his second son, David, was born. David was only a few months old when Abe contracted polio, which kept him at home for six months.

When he had recovered, more or less, the family decided on a move to Hibbing, an iron-mining town up near the Canadian border which had been Beatty's home before her marriage. Both sides of her family, the Stones and the Edelsteins, were established there. A community of about 17,000 people, mostly from eastern and southern Europe, the town had been ravaged first by lumbermen and then by open-cast mining, which tore huge chunks out of the countryside wherever iron ore was found close to the surface. As with all mining towns, its prosperity fluctuated according to market forces. Now Abe Zimmerman joined two of his brothers in a furniture and electrical goods business, while the family moved in with Beatty's parents.

It is not hard to imagine Bob, a slight, quiet, round-faced boy, on the fringes of adolescent social life in this industrious, tradition-minded Iron Range town in the mid-fifties. He was just into his teens when *The Blackboard Jungle* and *Rebel Without a Cause* came to town, casting their powerful spell on the imaginations of boys and girls for whom following their parents' example wasn't going to be enough. 'Bob was different,' Echo Helstrom, his first serious girlfriend, once said. 'Mostly, he withdrew inside himself, a silent kind of rebellion.' He liked cowboy

AFTER ABE ZIMMERMAN LOST HIS JOB WITH STANDARD OIL IN DULUTH, HE MOVED THE FAMILY TO HIBBING. AFTER LIVING WITH BEATTY'S PARENTS FOR THE FIRST FEW YEARS, IN 1952 THEY MOVED INTO THIS FAMILY HOUSE ON SEVENTH AVENUE IN THE FAIRVIEW ADDITION NEIGHBOURHOOD.

© JEFF SYME

When James Dean came to Hibbing in 1956, on the cinema screen in *Rebel Without a Cause*, Bobby Zimmerman found a hero and a role-model. Soon his bedroom walls were covered with pictures of the young actor.

Following Hank Williams, Johnny Ray and Bill Haley, Elvis Presley was the key musical figure in the teenage Dylan's life. After Presley's death in 1977, Dylan 'didn't talk to anyone for a week'.

stories, but there were pictures of James Dean on his bedroom walls.

It was the unselfish diligence and thrift of millions of Abe and Beatty Zimmermans that made possible the rebellion of a Bob Dylan. Their success in building a life in their community permitted him the luxury of dreams; their adherence to a narrowly defined set of social conventions – necessary to sustain a measure of prosperity in their lives – created something against which their son could react, something for him to test and push to breaking point. You can be a rebel without a cause, but you can't be a rebel without something to leave behind, and the quiet, industrious life of the Zimmermans provided the platform.

By many people's standards, Bob had a privileged adolescence: he was eleven or twelve when the success of Zimmerman Furniture and Electric provided funds for a turquoise Sears Roebuck mail-order guitar, on which he started to bang out the Hank Williams hillbilly ballads that had caught his attention on the radio and on the record-players of friends and relatives; at fifteen, he got a five-year-old Harley Davidson motorcycle. Sometime between these two events he'd seen

James Dean and started listening to black radio stations beaming rhythm-and-blues records in from distant Shreveport, Louisiana, and Little Rock, Arkansas. While most of Hibbing's teenagers were listening to Pat Boone and Patti Page, Bob heard Johnny Ace's 'Pledging My Love', Chuck Berry's 'Maybellene' and Little Walter's 'My Babe'.

This is how the white rock of the sixties – of the Beatles and the Rolling Stones – was born, among isolated schoolboys in the mid-1950s responding intuitively to what seemed a set of secret codes, learning them by heart (listening to the radio with the sound turned down while the parents and older siblings watched TV, haunting the local record store on the way home from school) and then, within a decade, taking those codes and turning them into a language.

Bob Zimmerman formed his first group, the Golden Chords, in 1955, when he was in junior high school. Monte Edwardson played guitar, Leroy Hoikkala played drums, and Bob played piano, guitar and harmonica and did the singing. They rehearsed in Abe Zimmerman's garage. Within weeks the Golden Chords were playing minor local functions and talent shows, but they disintegrated in the autumn when Bob fell under a new spell. Joining Johnny Ace and Fats Domino on the black stations was a newer, wilder voice: twenty-year-old Richard Penniman, Little Richard, the first man to blend the ecstatic trance of Holiness Church worship with the song structures and content of rhythm and blues. 'Tutti Frutti' and 'Long Tall Sally' were being played on the radio, obliterating the competition in a blast of screaming, pounding craziness.

Bob Zimmerman piled and greased his hair into a pompadour, practised hammering fast triplets with his right hand at the top end of the piano keyboard, and pushed his larynx into an approximation of Richard's abandoned shriek. When the other members of the Golden Chords protested, he simply left them behind.

His next band doesn't seem to have had a name, but he was able to mould it into a

PRESLEY OCCUPIED THE MIDDLE GROUND BETWEEN DEAN'S EXISTENTIAL COOL AND THE TOTAL ABANDON OF LITTLE RICHARD, WHOM THE YOUNG PIANO-PLAYING DYLAN COPIED IN HIS FIRST HIGH-SCHOOL GROUPS.

ROW 1: John Milinovich, Mike Minelli, Bob Zimmerman, Frank Sherman. ROW 2: Pat Lamprecht, Carole Del Grande, Marsha Banen, Verlene Carpenter, Bonnie Schoenig, Sally Jolowsky, Carol Tappero, Mary Jane Svigel. ROW 3: Pierina Maracchini, Helen Taylor, Colleen Schulz, Barbara Rostvold, Barbara Satovich, Darlene Solinger, Jean Wright, Donna Urbia, Pat Baumgardner.

HIBBING HIGH SCHOOL FOUND DYLAN A PUPIL OF ORIGINAL THOUGHTS BUT PATCHY CONCENTRATION. IN 1956, AT THE SCHOOL'S ANNUAL TALENT FESTIVAL, HIS FOUR-PIECE BAND SCANDALIZED TEACHERS AND PARENTS IN A CLASSIC SCENARIO OF EARLY ROCK AND ROLL.

closer approximation of his new idols. At Hibbing High School's annual talent festival, in a scene that could have come from *The Blackboard Jungle,* their amplified rock 'n' roll scandalized teachers and parents just the way it was supposed to. The adults clapped their hands to their ears and retreated to the rear, the principal ran backstage and told the janitor to cut the electricity, the girls tittered and the boys tried not to look envious of the musicians, who had suddenly established themselves as something more than mere classmates.

One day late in 1957, seventeen-year-old Bob Zimmerman met sixteen-year-old Echo Helstrom in a café on Hibbing's main street. He'd been playing with his band in the upstairs room; now he struck up a conversation and played her a few songs on his guitar. She had long blonde hair, blue jeans and a motorcycle jacket; she said she listened to the same black music on the same radio stations, and she turned out to have dreams like his. A month later, they were going steady, riding round Hibbing on his Harley in their leather jackets, talking music, and listening to the collection of hillbilly records kept by Echo's mother at the Helstrom house three miles out of town.

There was tension

surrounding the relationship from the start: Abe Zimmerman was a respected member of the community with a substantial family home (although prevented, as a Jew, from joining the golf club), whereas Matt Helstrom was an odd-job man whose house wasn't much more than a shack.

At first, the contrast between their backgrounds drew Bob and Echo together. Never a serious candidate for the Rotary Club or the Junior Chamber of Commerce, Bob was already developing an affinity for outsiders and outcasts – and even in Hibbing there were plenty around. He'd been shocked when his father had sent him to repossess goods purchased on credit by local people who'd lost their jobs in a slump, and the sound of the blues records on the radio was making him aware of the existence of black people and their culture. There were, in fact, practically no blacks in Minnesota's mining towns in the 1950s; the cheap labour had been provided by Europe's poor. But Bob was reading John Steinbeck now, and he could see, in the sadness of the small, unfulfilled, powerless lives in the remote North Country, how the great dream had gone sour at its margins. So he had no social scruples about dating a girl who might

not have been his parents' idea of a good match; indeed, he needed someone who could feed his visions of a life beyond Hibbing, beyond Minnesota – a life that he'd decided only his guitar could give him.

Echo followed him through the early months of 1958, as he fitted appearances with his now ever-changing parade of bands (the Shadow Blasters, the Satin Tones and Elston Gunn and the Rock Boppers were some of the names they went under) around the increasingly unalluring requirements of Hibbing High School. But he was moving on, beginning to widen his horizons with weekend trips to Duluth and Minneapolis/St Paul, and the relationship began to suffer from the friction between her desire for a settled partnership and his visions of something over the horizon.

It was at this time that he began to try on other identities. With images of Dean and Presley and Little Richard flashing inside his head, a boyhood in the comfortable house of a store-owning Rotarian didn't seem half colourful enough to present to the world. So the gigs and the road trips and the conversations with strangers began to assume the quality of experiments in living. Every

HIS JUNIOR HIGH SCHOOL YEARBOOK, 1958.

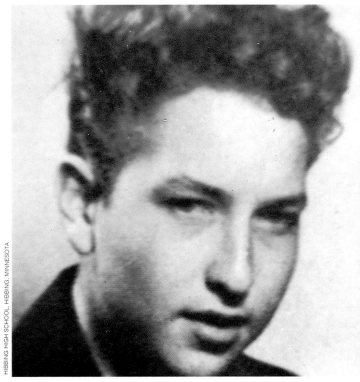

HIBBING HIGH SCHOOL, HIBBING, MINNESOTA

time he left Hibbing and travelled the 200 miles down Highway 61 to Minneapolis, he was adding a layer to his self-created myth. And these layers formed both a shield and a decoration, something to attract people, but also to keep them at a distance, lest they discover the mundane reality. This, perhaps, is when the agony of stardom begins — with the first exaggeration, the first distortion, the first pure invention, the first attempt to put some distance between the private person and the public one. As essential as these elements may be both in the development of an arresting image and, more subtly, in the creation of the art itself, in the end every last one becomes a burden — and the more there are, the more excruciating and inescapable the agony. We can count with some accuracy what his self-invention has earned Robert Allen Zimmerman, but we can only guess at what it

has cost him.

Bob started telling stories about himself. He said he got the name Dillon – as he first spelt it – from his mother's brother, a gambler, but that wasn't true. There were Dillons in Hibbing, and there was a Dillon on TV: Matt Dillon, the heroic lawman in *Gunsmoke.* Bobby Dillon, Bob Dillon; it was a strong, simple name, an American name – maybe a name to put up next to Buddy Holly, Eddie Cochran, Ricky Nelson, Don and Phil Everly.

Bob and Echo split up in the summer of 1958, as he got more serious about music and

HOWARD STREET, HIBBING'S MAIN DRAG, IN THE LATE 1940S: HERE WAS WHERE THE YOUNG DYLAN HAUNTED MUSIC SHOPS, AND WHERE, AT THE L & B CAFÉ, HE MET ECHO HELSTROM.

HIBBING HIGH SCHOOL, HIBBING, MINNESOTA

HIS SENIOR HIGH SCHOOL YEARBOOK, 1959.

keener to spend time away from Hibbing. Now he had a little band in Duluth, where he played at the weekends; with another, he made a TV appearance in Superior, across the state line in Wisconsin. And on a January night in 1959 he went to see Buddy Holly at Duluth Armory, as part of the three-week package tour of the Midwest billed as the Winter Dance Party. Buddy Holly, twenty-two years old, had already enjoyed eighteen months of fame. In 'That'll Be the Day' and 'Peggy Sue', Bob Zimmerman heard the sort of musicianly blend of country music with rhythm and blues he'd been hankering after, along with some of the teen appeal to which he ardently aspired.

As far as the performers were concerned, the Winter Dance Party was one big drag — Holly complained in a phone call to his young wife back home in New York that the band's coach was cold and dirty and the facilities poor — but for a seventeen-year-old high school senior with rock 'n' roll in his heart, it was a revelation.

Then, five days after the Duluth show, the single-engined Beechcraft carrying Holly, Ritchie Valens and the Big Bopper came down only a couple of minutes out of Mason City, Iowa — 150 miles south of Minneapolis — killing the singers and their pilot. They'd been on their way to a show in Fargo, North Dakota, where the promoter called up a local band to replace them. This band, the Shadows, included the three Velline brothers — one, the singer, called himself Bobby Vee.

Bob Zimmerman graduated from Hibbing High on 5 June 1959; the picture caption in his yearbook recorded his ambition: 'To join Little Richard'. Although the shadows of college enrolment were closing in, he spent the summer trying to make progress towards his aim.

He went to Fargo, where he worked as a waiter in a coffee-house and came to the attention of the Velline brothers, who were thinking about adding a piano-player to the Shadows. According to Bobby Vee, Bob lied about his professional experience, asked to be known as Elston Gunn, and played a couple of local dances with the band before the brothers decided they couldn't afford an extra musician. Only a few weeks later, Vee and the Shadows were creeping into the national charts with a song called 'Suzy Baby', enabling their erstwhile pianist to add a suitably enhanced version of the brief association to his expanding personal mythology. The following year, the clean-cut Vee took 'Rubber Ball' into the top ten and became an international pop star.

As the summer ended, Robert Allen Zimmerman found himself fulfilling his parents' wishes by enrolling at the University of Minneapolis, pledging allegiance to a Jewish fraternity house and, at least to begin with, attending English classes. The best thing about Minneapolis was the instant access to the ready-made coffee-house social life, most of which was centred on a district called Dinkytown. This was where the local Bohemians of the late fifties congregated. They were the last flowering of the Beat Generation, the sort of people still fired by Jack Kerouac and Lenny Bruce, Zen and Existentialism; still holding jazz-and-poetry concerts and happenings; still wearing baggy sweaters and goatees; mimicking the Greenwich Village of the early fifties (itself a mimicry of the Left Bank). It was, Bob Dylan said many years later, 'just like the stories you hear – free love, wine, poetry, nobody had any money . . .' Introducing his literary anthology *The Beat Scene* in March 1960, the New York-based writer Elias Wilentz observed: 'Now in the mid-twentieth century, at a time of the country's greatest economic prosperity, has come again the Bohemian discovery of the insignificance of wealth.

The Bohemian lives by his ideas and emotions . . . Of explicit political attitudes, a deep suspicion and distrust of all state operations and participation dominates a rejection of both armed camps – communist and capitalist . . .' This was just what Bob Zimmerman had been looking for.

It was also the fertile seedbed of the folk music revival, providing a new audience for the music of Woody Guthrie, Pete Seeger and the Weavers, whose songs dealt with crimes against minorities and working men, with injustice and oppression. Here was a territory that the emerging Bob Dillon could work in, listening to new acquaintances and passing strangers, picking up pieces of knowledge – reading 'The Waste Land', learning how to make a rudimentary harmonica holder – and adding features to his emerging self-image.

Here he could turn his carefully scraped-together knowledge of folk and blues music into a real currency. He started off playing a coffee-house in St Paul called the Purple Onion, but the principal location for the local beats was a Dinkytown coffee-house called the Ten o'Clock Scholar. In February 1960 he took up a weekend residency there, falling in with another

guitarist and singer, 'Spider' John Koerner, an ex-Marine who had gone back to high school in Minneapolis. To begin with, the two traded songs and sometimes played duets. But after three months, when Bob demanded a rise from three to five dollars a night (Koerner was getting four dollars), the proprietor refused and he went back to the Purple Onion.

By the spring he had virtually given up his studies; by autumn his formal education was over. He was out of the fraternity house – whose relationship with the surly, wilful eighteen-year-old had

REX FEATURES

BOBBY VEE, ANOTHER MINNESOTA BOY, SANG WITH THE BAND THAT TOOK BUDDY HOLLY'S SLOT IN FARGO, NORTH DAKOTA, ON THE NIGHT AFTER HOLLY'S PLANE WENT DOWN IN FEBRUARY 1959. A FEW MONTHS LATER, DYLAN PLAYED TWO DANCES IN FARGO AS PIANIST WITH VEE'S BAND.

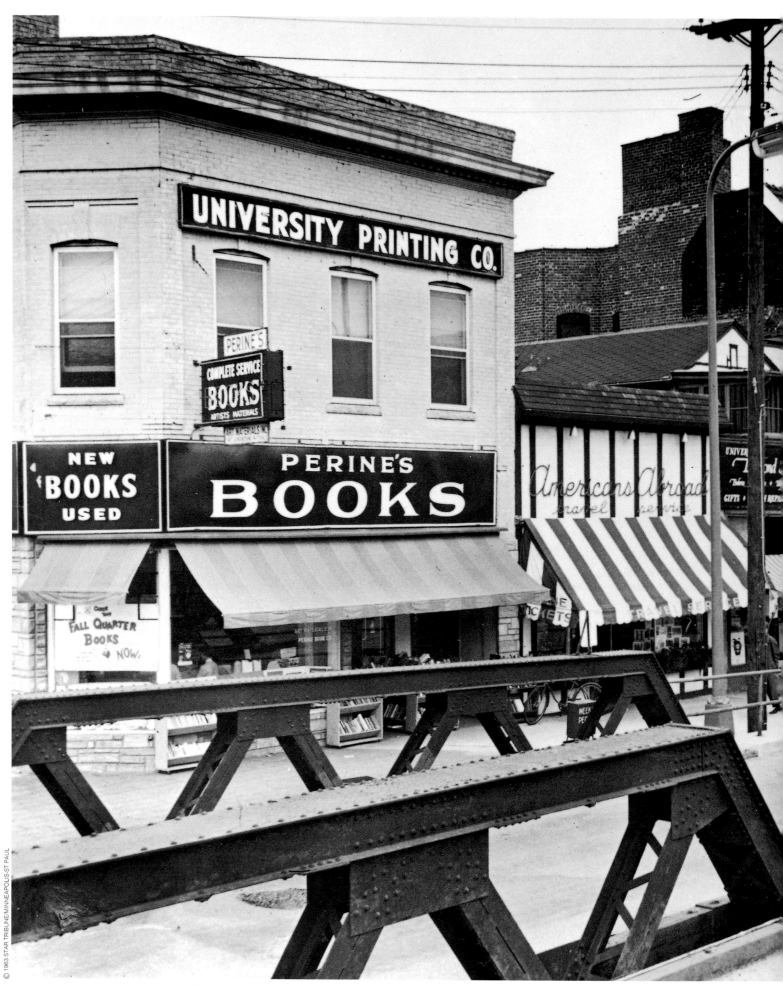

been difficult from the start — and into a series of cheap apartments. University hadn't been the reality he wanted; that was to be found in the carnival of 'poets and painters, drifters, scholarly types, experts at one thing and another who had dropped out of the regular nine-to-five life . . . most everybody, anyway, you had the feeling that they'd just been kicked out of something.' These were the people with whom he could discover *On the Road*, *Howl*, *Nova Express*: ' "I saw the best minds of my generation destroyed by madness" — that said more to me than any of the stuff I'd been raised on.'

Drinking wine and smoking dope, he listened to Leadbelly, Odetta and Jimmy Reed, and wrote his first song — a blues called 'One-Eyed Jacks', which shared its title with a Marlon Brando movie set in turn-of-the-century Mexico. With Koerner and a couple more singers, Tony Glover and Dave Ray, he studied and learnt and practised what he found.

DINKYTOWN WAS MINNEAPOLIS'S
GREENWICH VILLAGE, AND WAS WHERE
DYLAN, WHO HAD ENROLLED AT THE
UNIVERSITY IN THE AUTUMN OF 1959,
LEARNT ABOUT JACK KEROUAC AND
WOODY GUTHRIE.

He had become quite an adept performer, popular at parties and – when he wasn't getting abusive with talkative audiences – in coffee-houses, by the time he made his most ambitious journey yet: a summer jaunt to Denver, almost a thousand miles away. There he failed an audition at a club called the Satire, played briefly at the Gilded Garter in nearby Central City, and hung around a Denver coffee-house called the Exodus, where he heard two performers who were to play a part in his development. The first of them was Jesse 'Lone Cat' Fuller, a Georgia-born one-man band who had travelled throughout the US before settling in the West in the 1920s. When Bob came across him in Denver, Fuller was sixty-four years old. Festooned with guitar, washboard, a home-made, foot-operated bass instrument called the 'fotdella' and a neck-slung rack containing a harmonica and a kazoo, he must have seemed like a figure from the most distant origins of Afro-American music. Not so much a blues singer as what was sometimes called a 'songster', he explored a varied repertoire which had as its highlight a jumpy, jokey, breathless song called 'San Francisco Bay Blues'. The mood of that song, like Fuller's flexible approach to music in general, was to live on in Bob Dylan's work. But if Jesse Fuller represented the best of the past, the possibilities of the future were embodied in Judy Collins, a twenty-one-year-old singer whose father had been a bandleader in the Rocky Mountain area. A former child prodigy of classical piano, she had developed a love of traditional folk music and was only a year away from recording her first album. Listening to her interpretations of songs like 'Maid of Constant Sorrow', he was impressed by her attitude to traditional material. This wasn't the dry, academic approach of the archivist; nor was it an attempt to turn oneself into a sixty-four-year-old sharecropper. It was a twenty-one-year-old making something new and moving of a shared heritage.

When he got back to Minneapolis at the end of the summer, Bob Dillon became Bob Dylan. Asked later on if

LONDON FEATURES INTERNATIONAL

A LIKING FOR ELVIS PRESLEY AND LITTLE RICHARD WAS NOTHING UNUSUAL FOR A TEENAGE BOY IN THE LATE FIFTIES, BUT IT WAS WHEN DYLAN ADDED THE INFLUENCE OF WOODY GUTHRIE THAT THE MIXTURE BECAME POTENT. ON HIS FIRST ALBUM, 'SONG TO WOODY' ESTABLISHED DYLAN'S CREDENTIALS.

he'd called himself after Dylan Thomas, the answer was no. It's understandable that he would want to disclaim such a close identification, but it's hard to believe that the Welsh poet's name didn't give him the inspiration.

More significantly, he made what was probably the single most important discovery of his life: he found Woody Guthrie, the poet of the dust bowl. A friend called Dave Whitaker, a Dinkytown boho, seems to have been the one to lend him a copy – itself borrowed from a university lecturer – of Guthrie's autobiography, *Bound for Glory*; instantly Dylan recognized someone from whom he could learn enough to flesh out the character he was creating. He sat in the Ten o'Clock Scholar until he'd finished it. 'I thought *Bound for Glory* was the first *On the Road*,' he was to say, 'and of course it changed my life like it changed everyone else's.'

Here he found an idol who told him that authority will screw you if it gets a chance, that only the poor are honest, and that all idols, including Woody Guthrie and, eventually, Bob Dylan, have feet of clay. Guthrie's songs – 'Grand Coulee Dam', 'Vigilante Man', 'This Land Is Your Land' – showed him that a white man could write and sing the blues, everyone's blues, with an

eloquence so direct that it was capable of shaping people's attitudes. 'I was completely taken over by him,' Dylan later said. 'He was like a guide.' Not least, Guthrie's example reinforced the image of the wandering troubadour that had been so attractive: yes, it confirmed, your only responsibility is to the songs. So complete was the conversion that Paul Nelson, a young journalist in Minneapolis who later became a respected rock critic, could write: 'It took him about a week to become the finest interpreter I have yet heard of the songs of Woody Guthrie.' Superficial elements of 'Woodyness' – the work shirts, the Oklahoma background – became part of the younger man's persona, but it was Guthrie's more profound qualities that were permanently absorbed. Dylan's first known recording, an informal tape made in the autumn of 1960, contains several Guthrie tunes, alongside traditional folk and blues material.

By this time, the forty-eight-year-old Guthrie was lying in a New Jersey hospital, halfway through a fifteen-year losing battle against Huntington's chorea. Bob was so taken by the whole situation, so moved by his new hero's plight, that he got the phone number of the hospital and tried to call from Dave Whitaker's apartment.

He began to fantasize about visiting the singer – to the point that, being Dylan, he even talked about having already met him.

In his mind, Bob had already left town. 'When I arrived in Minneapolis, it seemed like a big city,' he was to say. 'When I left, it was like some rural outpost that you see once from a passing train.' Hitching rides, carrying only a suitcase and a guitar, he headed for his destiny – but not before stopping off in Hibbing to tell his folks what he was up to, and to pocket a little family subsidy.

First he went to Chicago, where he stayed with a folk singer he'd met in Denver, and then on to Madison, Wisconsin. But Greenwich Village seemed a long way away, and he grew discouraged; suddenly the familiarity of Minneapolis had its attractions. He looked for a lift back – and found himself instead with the offer of a ride to New York with another singer, Fred Underhill, as relief drivers for a couple of college students.

And so, one late-January day in 1961, as the snow lay deep in the worst winter for sixty years, a car crossed the George Washington Bridge into Manhattan and stopped by the kerb. The door opened. Bob Dylan, twenty years old, had arrived in New York.

2. chimes of freedom

© 1992 JIM MARSHALL

'I played all the
folk songs with
a rock and roll
attitude'

 What Dylan did first was head for Greenwich Village. This was it: here was the place and here were the people of which Dinkytown and its denizens were a pale copy. Here was the scene.

At the Café Wha? on Bleecker Street, he talked his way in to see the manager, Manny Roth, and asked to play. That night, wearing the clothes he'd travelled in, with his black corduroy cap on his curly hair and his harmonica holder round his neck, he made his New York début. A half-full house seems to have enjoyed it – to the extent that when Manny Roth asked the audience if anyone could put the new arrival up for the night, there was no shortage of offers.

The very next day, Dylan headed straight for the Greystone Park Hospital in New Jersey, where the palsied Woody Guthrie lay, barely able to move or talk. Dylan paid nervous homage, sang a few items from his considerable repertoire of Guthrie's songs at the bedside, and made the discovery that his hero was allowed out at weekends to visit the East Orange home of

two longtime fans, Bob Gleason and his wife Sid. Dylan made for the Gleason house, where he was told that he'd be welcome to come back and visit at the weekend, when Guthrie would be there.

Here, straight away, within hours of his arrival on the East Coast, was the entrée he needed. The Gleasons' place had become a rendezvous for some of the most admired folk singers in the Guthrie tradition: the likes of Pete Seeger, Cisco Houston and Ramblin' Jack Elliott were regular visitors, taking part in informal sessions which the Gleasons taped on their domestic recording equipment, compiling what would eventually become a remarkable archive.

Dylan's charm – a blend of

homespun innocence and winsome humour which seems to have cast him as something of a cross between Huckleberry Finn and Charlie Chaplin – endeared him to this new circle of friends; to begin with, at least, he must have been sufficiently awed to restrict the biting sarcasm that was also part of his nature. Within a fortnight, Dylan had sent an ecstatic postcard to Dave Whitaker in Dinkytown: 'I know Woody . . . I know Woody and met him and saw him and sang to him. I know Woody – goddamn. Dylan.'

A more profound response was to sit down and write his first substantial composition. In 'Song to Woody', Dylan was making several important connections: to its dedicatee and the anti-establishment

THE CAFÉ WHA? ON MACDOUGAL STREET IN GREENWICH VILLAGE, WHERE MANNY ROTH GAVE DYLAN AND MANY OTHER YOUNG FOLK SINGERS A CHANCE TO TEST THEMSELVES.

stance he represented; to the world of folk music (in a double gesture, Dylan set his original lyric for 'Song to Woody' to a traditional tune which had already been recycled by Guthrie as '1913 Massacre'); and – in its closing verse – to any people of his own age who might be listening. It doesn't undermine the seriousness of the song to suggest that 'I'm a-leavin' tomorrow, but I could leave today' is the statement of a troubadour who wants the girls to know that this could be their only chance.

'Hard Times in New York Town' was another of the dozen or so songs he wrote in 1961, and no doubt there were bleak days that year. But it can't have been so bad. Various couples he met at coffee-house hootenannies put him up in their apartments; they seem to have been older people, seduced by his youth and apparent helplessness and

AFTER GUTHRIE, PETE SEEGER WAS THE LEADER OF THE FOLK-PROTEST MOVEMENT. HE BECAME AN IMPORTANT EARLY CHAMPION OF DYLAN, OFTEN PERFORMING THE YOUNGER MAN'S SONGS.

© 1961 FRED W. MCDARRAH

seeing themselves as surrogate parents. There was, too, no shortage of younger women who listened to his stories and were anxious to get to know the young man who might or might not have been an orphan from Oklahoma, might or might not have played piano with Bobby Vee, might or might not have known Woody Guthrie personally since he was thirteen years old, might or might not have spent years working in carnivals down Texas way, might or might not have picked up his bottleneck guitar technique from an old black singer in New Mexico.

Nor, in a boom time for young folk musicians, was Bob Dylan destined to spend much time giving his talent for nothing. At the beginning of April he played his first paid engagement in the city, for the New York University Folk Music Society at the Loeb Student Center; two days earlier he had joined the

One night early in 1961, Dylan joined the singers Karen Dalton and Fred Neil on stage at the Café Wha?: 'There was not such a thing as an audience — /There was not such a thing as performers — /Everybody did somethin' — /And had somethin' t' say about somethin' . . .'

union, the American Federation of Musicians. But his real break came when Mike Porco, the owner of Gerde's Folk City, which had opened on West 4th Street that February, let him play for nothing at one of the popular Monday night hootenannies – after making him bring along proof that he was over eighteen. Porco, evidently impressed, followed up by giving Dylan a residency from 11 to 24 April as the supporting attraction to a bona fide legend: John Lee Hooker, the great Mississippi-born blues singer and guitarist. Naturally, Hooker got what publicity was going, but Porco noted how hard the younger man worked to put himself across for not much more than the union minimum payment of $90 a week.

In May, after four months of securing a foothold in New York, he played his first folk festival: a small event in the grounds of a hotel at Branford, Connecticut. He sang several Guthrie songs, and was introduced to another young singer, Bob Neuwirth, who was to become a firm friend. Now he was on the move.

A few days later he went back to Minneapolis to play at the university. His old friends heard a more confident performer than the boy who'd left in December, with a richer

repertoire and, more importantly, a personal style. He'd learnt from the bluesmen, from the hillbillies, from Guthrie's dustbowl ballads. He knew that a song with a story could hold an audience, and that you didn't need to sing like Caruso to put it over as long as you had character and emotion in your voice.

While he may have looked two or three years younger than his age, everything about his delivery – the raw, abraded vocal tone, the skilful combination of strumming and finger-picking, the wailing harmonica style adapted from Jimmy Reed and Sonny Terry – sounded prematurely aged. When he sang 'House of the Rising Sun' in a stretched-out arrangement taught to him by a more experienced Village singer, Dave Van Ronk, he sounded like he'd spent a lifetime sitting in the parlour of a New Orleans whorehouse, learning everything there was to learn about life. The apocalyptic imagery of the old bluesmen carried a fresh charge of potency when it came from the mouth of this very young white man; he borrowed 'See that My Grave Is Kept Clean' from Blind Lemon Jefferson, but he gave it the nightmarish intensity associated with Robert Johnson, the shadowy pre-war blues singer who had allegedly sold his soul to the devil in exchange for his unearthly talent before being poisoned by a girlfriend's jealous husband in 1938, at the age of twenty-seven. Dylan could also take the plaintive ballads of the Appalachians, with their gallery of archetypal stories and characters going back to Elizabethan times, and animate them in a way that made the songs into more than mere exhibits in the museum of folk music. What was now obvious was that, while he had a rare gift for absorbing existing styles and ideas, he was beholden to none of his sources: a straight twelve-bar blues or a modal English minuet took on the same voice, each equally freighted with the strange, unspoken wisdom of this boy barely out of his teens.

Back in New York in June, he was hired for his first recording session, as an accompanying musician. Harry Belafonte, the featured artist, represented the mainstream of the folk boom: a black singer thought by the purists to have sold out to the commercial desires of his record company. At the RCA studios in New York, Dylan played harmonica on 'Midnight Special' — a traditional prisoner's lament — but seems to have disliked the formal nature of the occasion and did not contribute to the session's other tracks. He was

learning from everything and everybody, though, and a brief visit to Boston resulted in another important friendship, with Eric Von Schmidt, a Connecticut-born illustrator and musician who taught him a couple of songs: 'Baby Let Me Follow You Down' and 'He Was a Friend of Mine'.

Three other vital relationships took shape that summer. The first was with Robert Shelton, a reviewer for the *New York Times*. Shelton had heard Dylan around the Village, and had found him interesting, but hadn't included him in his notices. Dylan began to pester him, and in July Shelton introduced him to Albert Grossman, an ambitious thirty-five-year-old music entrepreneur who had begun as a singer himself, had managed Odetta — a singer admired by Dylan — and had launched the eighteen-year-old Joan Baez at the Newport Folk Festival in 1959; he was now in the middle of putting together a group called Peter, Paul and Mary in an attempt to emulate the recent success of the Kingston Trio, with folk music harmonized and sanitized for the mass market. And then, one Monday night at Gerde's Folk City, Bob Dylan came under the scrutiny of an eighteen-year-old girl called Susan Rotolo.

Born into a politically active New York family, Suze Rotolo

WHEN PETE SEEGER CAME BACK FROM A VISIT TO ENGLAND IN 1961, HE DECIDED TO FOUND A RADICAL FOLK-SONG MAGAZINE AS A FOCAL POINT FOR YOUNG WRITERS AND PERFORMERS. DYLAN'S 'TALKIN' JOHN BIRCH PARANOID BLUES' WAS PUBLISHED IN THE FIRST ISSUE OF *BROADSIDE* IN FEBRUARY 1962, AND HE WAS A REGULAR ATTENDER AT THE MEETINGS OF ITS EDITORIAL COLLECTIVE THAT YEAR.

and her older sister Carla had been listening to Leadbelly and Woody Guthrie since infancy. They were already involved in the protest movement – against McCarthyism, against nuclear weapons, against segregation. By her teens, Suze was going to Washington Square at the weekends to listen to singers serenading an open-air audience. When she heard Dylan, who was playing in a duo with Mark Spoelstra, she was already a regular in the Village folk clubs. First of all, she was to say later, she fell for his harmonica-playing. They met, they talked, they met again – at parties, at other hootenanny nights. By the end of the summer they were a couple.

In September, Mike Porco gave Dylan another fortnight at Folk City, this time supporting the Greenbriar Boys (specialists in bluegrass music), billed as 'the sensational Bob Dylan'. After

SUZE ROTOLO WAS EIGHTEEN WHEN SHE MET BOB DYLAN IN 1961. TWO YEARS LATER SHE WAS TO BE FOUND ARM IN ARM WITH HIM ON WEST 4TH STREET, IN THE *FREEWHEELIN'* COVER SHOT THAT HELPED SHAPE A GENERATION'S DREAMS.

musing for several weeks, Bob Shelton had decided that now was the time to make Bob Dylan's existence known to his readership. He came down on opening night, and wrote a review which appeared in the *New York Times* on 29 September. Headlined 'Bob Dylan: A Distinctive Folk-Song Stylist' across three columns in the sober style which the *Times* preserves to this day, and accompanied by a small photograph, it was a piece that would be hard to beat for sheer prescience. 'Mr Dylan's voice is anything but pretty,' Shelton wrote. 'He is consciously trying to recapture the rude beauty of a Southern field hand musing in melody on his porch. All the "husk and bark" are left on his notes and a searing intensity pervades his songs . . . At times, the drama he aims at is off-target melodrama and his stylization threatens to topple over as a mannered excess . . . But if not for every taste, his music-making has the mask of originality and inspiration, all the more noteworthy for his youth. Mr Dylan is vague about his antecedents and birthplace, but it matters less where he has been than where he is going, and that would seem to be straight up.'

No matter how justifiably cynical an artist may become as critics pile carelessness upon misunderstanding in the course of a career, usually there is a point at which a good review turns the key. This was that point for Bob Dylan. He clipped out Shelton's words and carried them with him for weeks, showing them around with pride. He could hardly be blamed: only two years out of high school, less than a year out of the hinterland, his name had appeared in an approving headline in the nation's leading daily newspaper.

Naturally enough, the reaction of his Greenwich Village friends and rivals was mixed; some felt it was part of a commercially motivated plot executed by Shelton at the behest of Grossman, who was continuing to show an interest in Dylan while taking Peter, Paul and Mary through a seven-month preparation for their own début. The guitarist Eric Weissberg was blunter: he told Shelton that he needed a hearing aid. Other people, though, took notice. A few days before the review appeared, Dylan had taken part in a rehearsal for a recording session by Carolyn Hester, a singer signed to Columbia Records in an attempt to match the growing success of Joan Baez. Dylan had met Hester and her husband, the writer Richard Fariña, during a trip to Cambridge, Massachusetts; now he was booked to provide harmonica accompaniment again and turned up for the rehearsal at an apartment on West 10th Street.

A tall, lean, neatly dressed fifty-year-old man with cropped grey hair was present when Dylan arrived. This was John Hammond, the legendary talent scout who had been instrumental in the careers of Count Basie, Bessie Smith, Billie Holiday, Charlie Christian and Benny Goodman. Unusually, Hammond had turned down the chance to sign Baez, letting her go instead to his former employer, the much smaller Vanguard label. Now he was trying to make amends. He noticed Dylan at the rehearsal, and paid even more attention to him at the recording session, which took place the day after the *New York Times* review appeared. As Dylan blew his harmonica over the fluent guitar of Bruce Langhorne and the double-bass of Bill Lee, Hammond didn't think his playing was particularly special, but he found himself intrigued by the boy's unusual presence. He'd read Shelton's review, and he invited Dylan to stop by Columbia's studios to show what he could do in his own right. In Hammond's own words: 'As it turned out, he had songs of his own. One was enough. He sang "Talking New York", a social commentary on life in Manhattan that knocked me out.' Within a month – having been turned down by three specialist folk labels, Elektra, Vanguard and Folkways – Bob Dylan was a Columbia Records artist, with a five-year contract binding him into a powerful roster which also included Pete Seeger, Miles Davis, Ray Conniff and Tony Bennett.

Hammond's immediate, intuitive response to Dylan was understandable in the light of his love of the blues and its offshoots. The child of a wealthy and socially active New York family (there were Vanderbilts on his mother's side), he had grown up in an eight-storey mansion just off Central Park but had dropped out of Yale to pursue his interest in music. He'd made many field trips to the South in search of obscure musicians in the thirties, and in 1938 he had presented Big Bill Broonzy and Sonny Terry alongside Sister Rosetta Tharpe and Count Basie at Carnegie Hall in a historic concert titled 'From Spirituals to Swing'; it was the first time such performers had appeared at the august venue. He had also long been active in the civil rights movement, and had something to do with the fact that, in 1936, the pianist Teddy Wilson became the first black musician to work in public with a white orchestra – that of Benny Goodman,

Hammond's brother-in-law.

Hammond was used to musicians and the problems posed by the way they lived, so it was natural for him to help the impecunious Dylan out with occasional small personal loans, a habit that would not come naturally to most record executives, then or now. He

also arranged for Dylan to sign a publishing deal with Leeds Music, for which the singer received a $500 advance against royalties.

Dylan had less than a month to prepare his first album. In the meantime, he was invited to play harmonica on another session, this time with the

veteran blues singers Victoria Spivey and Big Joe Williams, on an album released on Spivey's own label under the title *Three Kings and a Queen*. The enthusiastic Spivey had heard Dylan at Gerde's, and responded to his requests for inclusion on one of her sessions. On 'Sitting on Top of

JOHN HAMMOND SR HAD KEEN A&R EARS AND A PRIVATE FORTUNE THAT ENABLED HIM TO HOLD ON TO HIS INTEGRITY. AFTER BESSIE SMITH, COUNT BASIE, BILLIE HOLIDAY, CHARLIE CHRISTIAN AND ARETHA FRANKLIN, HE FOUND HIMSELF INTRIGUED BY A SCRUFFY YOUNG FOLK SINGER FROM MINNESOTA. HERE THEY ARE AT AN EARLY RECORDING SESSION IN COLUMBIA'S STUDIOS AT 799 SEVENTH AVENUE, NEW YORK CITY.

MICHAEL OCHS ARCHIVES

the World', Dylan even sang back-up, trading call-and-response phrases with the battle-scarred Williams.

On Saturday 4 November, Dylan gave his first solo concert, at Carnegie Chapter Hall. It was promoted by his friend Izzy Young, who ran the New York Folklore Center and was a hub of the Village scene; somewhere in the background, Albert Grossman was providing encouragement. Admission to the small recital room was two dollars, and although a mere fifty-three people turned up (most of whom were used to hearing him in the Village clubs), Dylan gave them a strong performance.

On 20 and 22 November he gave an even better performance. In two three-hour sessions, at a cost in studio time and magnetic tape of just $402, Bob Dylan recorded the thirteen songs that were to make up his first album. He showed up at the Columbia studios on Seventh Avenue with Suze in tow; Hammond, who was to produce the session, brought along Goddard Leiberson, the president of Columbia Records and an eminent figure in the world of classical music. For the president of a large record company to attend the first session of a novice signing would be rare at any time, and this was a remarkable augury.

Heeding Hammond's tips on

microphone technique, Dylan moved fast through the sort of set he delivered in the clubs: Jesse Fuller's 'You're No Good', the traditional 'Pretty Peggy-O', Van Ronk's arrangement of 'House of the Rising Sun', Von Schmidt's 'Baby Let Me Follow You Down' and two originals, 'Talking New York' and 'Song to Woody'. Hammond was

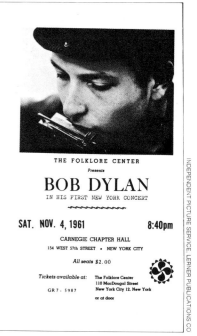

THE POSTER FOR DYLAN'S FIRST SOLO CONCERT, WHICH ATTRACTED AN AUDIENCE OF FIFTY-THREE FOLK-MUSIC DEVOTEES. HIS REPERTOIRE INCLUDED SONGS BY BUKKA WHITE, LEADBELLY, WOODY GUTHRIE AND BESSIE SMITH.

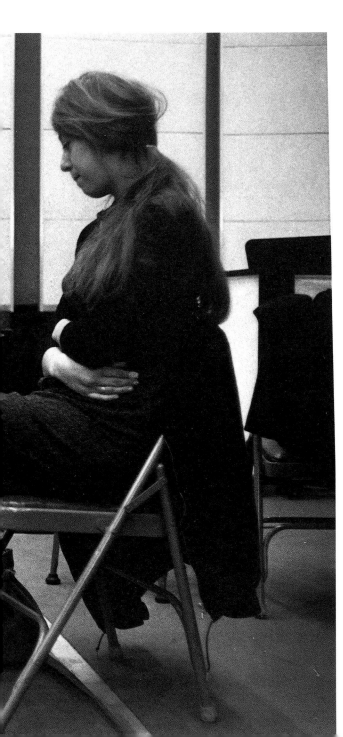

WITH SUZE IN COLUMBIA'S STUDIO A, REHEARSING FOR HIS FIRST ALBUM IN LATE NOVEMBER 1961.

impressed by Dylan's sheer willingness to get on with it, and by the fact that each song needed only a handful of takes – none more than five, some completed in two. Throughout the sessions, Dylan sounded alert and confident, at home with his material and able to vary his guitar technique to get the best out of the songs. On 'Highway 51' and 'Man of Constant Sorrow', in particular, he showed an unusual gift for timing, building tension by holding a strumming pattern between the lines of the lyric or sustaining a note in a way learnt from the blues singers. As well as the raw tone of his voice, the stresses and distortions he made – many of them conveying a sense of playfulness – were a shock to ears accustomed to the clarity of conventional interpreters. And then there was his harmonica, which mixed the long, lonesome whistling notes of a Jimmy Reed with an enthusiastic chuffing that seemed all his own, and which sometimes (as in the fast-paced 'Gospel Plow') worked as a kind of two-part invention with his guitar-playing. The fact that Dylan played the harmonica from a neck-harness meant that he couldn't bend notes as powerfully as bluesmen like Little Walter or Sonny Terry; this, too, helped give him an original sound.

But the prevailing mood of the album was really defined by three old blues songs dealing with a single subject: Blind Willie Johnson's 'In My Time of Dyin'', Bukka White's 'Fixin' to Die' and Blind Lemon Jefferson's 'See that My Grave Is Kept Clean'. Here all traces of the engaging, playful, sometimes comic club performer dropped away. Here a twenty-year-old boy was getting under the skin of some of the most obsessed songs written in the English language. Dylan was paying homage to Johnson, White and Jefferson, but he wasn't pretending to be them. The ferocity of his parched young voice and the whining of his open-tuned guitar made something different of the bluesmen's apocalyptic fatalism; there was a sense of youthful foreboding that spoke directly to a new generation that had grown up in a confusion of post-war consumer prosperity and the Cold War rhetoric of mutually assured destruction. The message, at this stage, was implicit: it was in the angry desolation of the voice, rather than the borrowed old words. But this, at the beginning of it all, was what riveted Dylan's younger listeners from the very first moment they heard him.

While he waited for Columbia to prepare the album

for release, he returned briefly to Minneapolis, this time with a dog-eared press clipping in his pocket and a forthcoming album to tell his friends about. When he got back to New York, he and Suze moved into an apartment on West 4th Street.

By the time *Bob Dylan* was released on 19 March 1962, Bob Dylan himself was somewhere else. Not many people bought the album, anyway. With a colour picture of an enigmatically half-smiling Dylan in his wandering-troubadour's cap and sheepskin coat on the cover, it achieved an initial sale of only about 5,000 copies, which certainly wasn't enough to make Dylan a significant earner for Columbia, or to justify Hammond's faith in the eyes of the accountants. In fact, to the younger executives at the company Dylan quickly became known as 'Hammond's folly', the embodiment of the lapsed judgement of a man who might once have had good ears but who had been bypassed by time and fashion.

Shortly after the new year, Dylan had written the first of a stream of songs protesting against injustice. 'The Death of Emmett Till' lamented the lynching, seven years earlier, of a fourteen-year-old black boy who had whistled at a white woman in Mississippi,

and the mockery of a trial that succeeded it. The song's inspiration was probably the imminence of Dylan's late-February appearance on the bill of a benefit concert for the Congress of Racial Equality — for which Suze was an enthusiastic voluntary worker. Set to a pattern of descending minor chords not unlike 'House of the Rising Sun', 'Emmett Till' built a powerful mood of regret and foreboding, with a minatory conclusion: 'If you can't speak out against this kind of thing, a crime that's so unjust, your eyes are filled with dead man's dirt and your mind is filled with dust . . .' Surviving only on a tape made for the radio station WBAI, it was a rough-edged blueprint for much of what was to follow.

There were other, similar songs: 'The Ballad of Donald White', inspired by a television interview with a black man on Death Row; 'Let Me Die in My Footsteps', which used the fall-out shelter as a symbol of Cold War madness. But within weeks of the unheralded release of his début album, Dylan was completing the song that was to provide the keystone of his international reputation. 'Blowin' in the Wind' was written at a table in the 4th Street apartment, in a booth of a coffee-house called the Commons, and probably at various other clubs and bars.

Its simple melody and gentle rhetoric, its uplifting images and its refusal (later much criticized) to offer solutions to the questions it posed made it the perfect song for its time. In May it was published in the sixth issue of *Broadside*, the magazine founded by Pete Seeger and devoted to topical songs. Almost immediately, it entered the repertoire of other Village singers.

Albert Grossman, more than anyone, could see what was happening. He knew that Dylan had a quality that was destined to move him beyond the confines of the folk scene. Grossman wasn't interested in coffee-houses and benefits: he had a vision of conquering the world. In the spring, he signed Dylan to a seven-year management contract and engineered the removal of his publishing rights from Leeds Music to Witmark and Sons, run by his friend Artie Mogull, who had heard 'Blowin' in the Wind' and recognized its potential. Mogull gave Dylan the money to buy himself out of the deal with Leeds, where a general lack of enthusiasm thereby cost the company an extremely lucrative publishing catalogue.

Grossman was disliked by many people during his long association with Dylan, but there isn't much doubt that his sharp business instincts and complete indifference to

'LARGE SELECTION OF MASKS': DYLAN ON 49TH STREET AT SEVENTH AVENUE, NEW YORK, 1962.

43

personal popularity were of considerable value to his artist. Grossman made sure people treated Dylan as though he were something special, not just another folk singer.

When Dylan and John Hammond embarked on the preparation for the second album, the producer soon discovered that he was fighting not only his enemies at Columbia but also his artist's new manager. Grossman and his assistants began to turn up at the sessions, offering advice on recording techniques to a man whose experience was second to none. While Hammond resented this interference, the sessions began well enough, with a session in July producing masters of 'Down the Highway', 'Honey Won't You Give Me One More Chance', and – in a performance of calculated restraint – 'Blowin' in the Wind'.

But something was wrong. Suze had left New York in June, urged by her mother and stepfather to study art in Italy and cut the ties with the unkempt boy from Minnesota, recording contract or no recording contract. Dylan was distraught. For six months, she had been his muse – his contact with the world of radical politics, his introduction to Rimbaud and Verlaine and Baudelaire and Bertolt Brecht. She had been

an integral part of everything that had happened to him.

While Suze was studying at the university of Perugia, Dylan poured his anguish into some of the finest love songs he has ever written, the first of which was the elegant, sorrowful 'Tomorrow Is a Long Time'. That was followed by 'Don't Think Twice, It's Alright', as complicated a statement of romantic loss as could be found. 'It isn't a love song,' Dylan said later. 'It's a statement that maybe you can say to make yourself feel better.' It may have been the first time that Dylan had rearranged elements of his own experience into a kind of semi-fiction. Some of 'Don't Think Twice' sounds like him talking to Suze, some of it sounds like her talking to Dylan, some of it may have been borrowed from other relationships altogether. Some of it may even have been pure invention. Perhaps this was the moment at which Dylan became simultaneously liable to analysis and resistant to it.

Suze's absence at least cleared a space for his songwriting, which accelerated until, by the end of the year, he was writing five or six songs a month, varying his style from the urgent, gospel-influenced drive of 'Quit Your Lowdown Ways' to the droning anti-establishment rant of 'Playboys and Playgirls' and

the topical humour of 'Talkin' John Birch Paranoid Blues'. His performing schedule was scanty: two short seasons at Gerde's in February and April-May, a weekend trip to Ann Arbor, Michigan, four days in Montreal, New York hootenannies at Carnegie Hall in September and Town Hall in October, and an engagement at the Gaslight Café in the Village in November were all that interrupted his composing and recording.

In Columbia's Seventh Avenue studios, the atmosphere wasn't improved when John Hammond heard that Albert Grossman was trying to get Dylan out of his Columbia contract, claiming that Dylan had been under-age when he signed it. That was true enough, but Dylan had told Hammond very firmly that he had no parents; Hammond now realized that, since Dylan had been back in the studios several times since his twenty-first birthday, he had automatically validated a contract signed when he was twenty. That was one round that Grossman lost – and the defeat may have strengthened his resolve to end Hammond's professional relationship with his artist.

Hammond was a purist. So was Dylan, when it came to other people. Dylan loved the pure blues of Big Joe Williams, the pure hillbilly songs of

Hank Williams, the pure bluegrass of Bill Monroe. When it came to himself, though, he was for miscegenation: he wanted to blend, to fuse, to find something that made all these things work together. He didn't want his blues to sound like Muddy Waters's blues, or Blind Gary Davis's, or Jimmy Reed's. He wanted his blues to sound like those of a twenty-one-year-old white boy who'd grown up not only with those people but also with Elvis Presley, Carl Perkins and Little Richard.

Twenty years later, Dylan was completely clear about what he had felt. Neither rock and roll nor folk music was enough to satisfy him. 'Tutti Frutti' and 'Blue Suede Shoes' were great catch-phrases and driving pulse rhythms and you could get high on the energy but they weren't serious or didn't reflect life in a realistic way, he said. 'I knew that when I got into folk music, it was more of a serious type thing. The songs were filled with more despair, more sadness, more triumph, more faith in the supernatural, much deeper feelings . . . Life is full of complexities, and rock and roll didn't reflect that.' On the other hand, he had no time for the 'strict and rigid establishment' of the folk scene who ordained that 'if you sang Texas cowboy songs, you didn't play English

Broadway and 52nd, in front of the Alvin Hotel, a favourite residence of jazz musicians in the days when 52nd was known as Swing Street.

ballads. It was pathetic.' Attitude, he concluded, was what he'd brought: 'I played all the folk songs with a rock and roll attitude. This is what made me different and allowed me to cut through all the mess and be heard.'

He made his first attempt to synthesize the two by bringing a rhythm section into the studio for two sessions in October and December – the first since he had legally changed his name to Bob Dylan in August. Hammond's hand was obvious in the choice of accompanists on these dates: mainstream jazz musicians with vast studio experience, accustomed to placing their skills at the service of a featured singer. Dylan had worked with the guitarist Bruce Langhorne before, on the Carolyn Hester session, but the others – including the pianist Dick Wellstood, the guitarist George Barnes, the bassists Leonard Gaskin and Gene Ramey, and the drummer Herb Lovelle – were from a different generation, and unable to respond with anything other than a session musician's dutiful professionalism. In 'Mixed-Up Confusion', released as his first single in December, you can hear Dylan trying to create something as wild as Jerry Lee Lewis's early Sun records, but with a surreal humour. Because none of the musicians

was pushing him, he failed completely. Hammond might have done better to give the production over to his own son, John Hammond Jr, a young white blues singer and guitarist around the Village who would have known instinctively the sort of energy Dylan was after.

In December, Dylan flew to London to take part in the recording of a BBC-TV play, Evan Jones's *The Madhouse on Castle Street*. Philip Saville, the play's adventurous English producer, was a friend of the folklorist Alan Lomax, and had heard Dylan in the Village the previous year. He made a deal with Grossman, flew Dylan over, and created a part for him as an anarchistic student. In fact, because Dylan wanted to rewrite all his lines, two parts were created: one was Dylan as he wanted to appear, the other was the original anarchistic student, now played by David Warner. Dylan sang two songs, 'Blowin' in the Wind' and the specially composed 'Ballad of the Gliding Swan'; the play went out on 13 January 1963, but the tape was wiped afterwards (common BBC policy at the time) and no record of the transmission now exists.

While rehearsing the play, Dylan also took the opportunity to check out the London folk scene. He sang at the Troubadour, the King &

AT THE END OF 1962, DYLAN CAME TO LONDON TO TAKE PART IN A BBC TELEVISION PLAY, EVAN JONES'S *MADHOUSE ON CASTLE STREET*. PLAYING THE PART OF BOBBY, A GUITAR-PLAYING HOBO EMBROILED IN A DOMESTIC DRAMA, HE SANG 'BLOWIN' IN THE WIND' AND 'BALLAD OF THE GLIDING SWAN'. THE PLAY WAS TRANSMITTED ON 12 JANUARY 1963, BUT NO TAPE WAS RETAINED.

Queen and the Singers' Club at the Pindar of Wakefield pub, to a mixed response: some of the die-hard traditionalists, such as Ewan MacColl and Peggy Seeger, thought him worthless, but younger performers and listeners were openly admiring. Dylan found a particular friend in Martin Carthy, a gifted singer-guitarist at whose house he stayed. From Carthy he learnt the traditional song 'Scarborough Fair'; from Nigel Denver, a Scottish singer with whom he had a drunken New Year's Day altercation at the

King & Queen, he picked up Dominic Behan's 'The Patriot Game'. At the Singers' Club, under the frosty gaze of Seeger and MacColl, he performed 'Masters of War', a blazing new diatribe against the military, and 'The Ballad of Hollis Brown', an extended piece of rural realism so vivid that it seemed like a series of snapshots, set against a pattern that sounded like the blues stripped back to its absolute essentials.

Dylan went to Italy for a few days – although Suze was already back in New York – and just before his return to the US he met up in London with Eric Von Schmidt and Richard Fariña. Joined by the fiddler Ethan Signer, they made a hurried and mildly inebriated album for the 77 label in a room at the back of Dobell's jazz record shop on Charing Cross Road. Dylan, who played harmonica on four tracks, was credited as 'Blind Boy Grunt' to avoid a conflict with his Columbia contract.

During his visit to London he made many friends among the younger British-based folk singers, but scandalized some older members of the folk establishment with performances like this one, at the Singers' Club in the Pindar of Wakefield pub on Gray's Inn Road on 22 December 1962.

WITH SUZE AND FRIENDS ON THE STREETS
OF NEW YORK CITY, EARLY 1963.

In the month of his return Dylan wrote a song which has always been among his best loved. 'Girl from the North Country' is based on the melody of 'Scarborough Fair', but its lyric has a completely original freshness. In later years it was taken to be a nostalgic address to Echo Helstrom. No doubt she inspired it, but to say that it was 'about' her would be to reduce a piece of art to the status of a jingle.

Minnesota was certainly on his mind, though, in the early weeks of 1963. 'Bob Dylan's Dream', written in February (and set to another Carthy-taught traditional melody, 'Lord Franklin'), may have been prompted by his return visits to Dinkytown and the friends with whom he had spent a formative year. For a twenty-one-year-old, this was a meditation of remarkable maturity. While sniffing the scent of success, he could look back on the days before contracts and royalty advances and say: 'Ten thousand dollars, at the drop of a hat/I'd give it all gladly if our lives could be like that.' It may not have been entirely true, but the fact that it could enter his mind was telling.

Now, too, he was reunited with Suze, and they tramped arm in arm through the snows of West 4th Street for the benefit of the Columbia Records photographer, whose touching colour shot became the evocative cover image for Dylan's second album. Suze was in the audience on 12 April, when he filled three-quarters of Town Hall's 900 seats for a solo concert which included an eight-minute poetic monologue titled 'Last Thoughts on Woody Guthrie'. Columbia's increasing interest in him was demonstrated by their decision to tape the concert, although it has never been released.

Before he left for England in December, Dylan had considered his second album complete. Now he changed his mind. In April, although promotional pressings of *The Freewheelin' Bob Dylan* had already been dispatched, he decided to replace four of the songs, apparently because he believed they inclined too much towards the character of the first album, too close to Woody Guthrie and the blues singers, and did not reflect the developments in his

songwriting. So out went 'Rocks and Gravel', 'Let Me Die in My Footsteps', 'Ramblin' Gamblin' Willie' and (probably to the record company's intense relief) the outspoken 'Talkin' John Birch Paranoid Blues'. In came four of his new songs, recorded in his usual solo-performer mode but with

a new man in the control booth. Tom Wilson, a young black record producer, had been brought in by Dave Kapralik, Columbia's head of pop A&R and John Hammond's principal foe. Wilson, who had recorded the avant-garde jazz musicians Cecil Taylor and Sun Ra for specialist labels, was

'She knows me well/Perhaps too well/An' is above all/The true fortuneteller of my soul/Perhaps the only one . . .'

SINGING 'ONLY A PAWN IN THEIR GAME', ABOUT THE MURDER OF MEDGAR EVERS, LEADER OF THE MISSISSIPPI NATIONAL ASSOCIATION FOR THE ADVANCEMENT OF COLORED PEOPLE, AT A CIVIL RIGHTS RALLY SURROUNDED BY COTTON FIELDS IN GREENWOOD, MISSISSIPPI. HERE, ON 6 JULY 1963, IN COMPANY WITH PETE SEEGER, DYLAN SAW SEGREGATION IN THE DEEP SOUTH AT FIRST HAND FOR THE FIRST TIME; HE HAD WRITTEN THE SONG TWO WEEKS EARLIER.

completely unfamiliar with folk music. 'I thought folk music was for the dumb guys,' he said. 'This guy played like the dumb guys, but then these words came out. I was flabbergasted.'

There wasn't much Tom Wilson needed to do to 'Girl from the North Country', 'Masters of War', 'Bob Dylan's Dream' and 'Talkin' World War III Blues'. Each of them was, in its way, perfect, and made a significant contribution to the impact of *Freewheelin'*, released on 27 May. The album was a notable advance on its predecessor: chiefly, it was a showcase for Dylan's own compositions, and even those who couldn't take the informal quality of his vocal delivery could see that here was someone with a real gift for words and music. For those with no such reservations, it was a recital almost dizzying in its scope and intensity, reaching a peak in the extraordinary 'A Hard Rain's A-Gonna Fall', about which Dylan somewhat archly told Nat Hentoff – the sleeve essayist – that every line was potentially the start of a new song 'but . . . I thought I wouldn't have enough time alive to write all those songs so I put all I could into this one.' As he piled symbol on symbol in 'Hard Rain' – setting them to the kind of hellish bleakness he'd learnt from Robert

THE APOTHEOSIS OF BOB DYLAN, FOLK SINGER, CAME ON 26 JULY 1963 AT FREEBODY PARK IN NEWPORT, RHODE ISLAND, WHEN HE SANG 'BLOWIN' IN THE WIND' AND WAS JOINED IN 'WE SHALL OVERCOME' BY PETER YARROW, MARY TRAVERS, PAUL STOOKEY, JOAN BAEZ, THE FREEDOM SINGERS, PETE SEEGER AND THEODORE BIKEL.

Johnson, mirroring the paranoia of the Cuban missile crisis – Dylan was laying the foundations of his entire cult. For students whose exam courses included Eliot and Yeats, here was something that flattered their expanding intellects while appealing to the teenage rebel in their early-sixties souls. James Dean had walked around reading James Joyce; here were both in a single package, the words and the attitude set to music.

No sooner had he and Suze appeared together in the record racks of America than Dylan met the next important woman in his life. At the end of May, at the Monterey Folk Festival in northern California, he was introduced to Joan Baez, by now the queen of the folk scene. Impressed by an advance pressing of *Freewheelin'*, she joined him on stage to sing a new song, 'With God on Our Side' – inspired by both the melody and the lyric content of 'The Patriot Game'. In July, Dylan sang a new civil rights song, 'Only a Pawn in Their Game', at a rally in Greenwood, Mississippi. Later in the month, his rising stature in the folk world was confirmed when he appeared with both Baez and Pete Seeger at the Newport Festival. Peter, Paul and Mary's version of 'Blowin' in the Wind' was already in the national pop charts. (It was to reach number two). When Dylan appeared with them, plus Baez, Pete Seeger, Theodore Bikel and the Freedom Singers, to close the festival's opening concert with 'We Shall Overcome', he had arrived as the movement's most potent new figure. 'He

© 1963 FRED W. MCDARRAH

HIS RELATIONSHIP WITH JOAN BAEZ WAS ALREADY UNDER WAY WHEN THEY SANG TOGETHER UNDER THE LINCOLN MEMORIAL DURING THE MARCH ON WASHINGTON ON 28 AUGUST 1963. A FEW MONTHS LATER, THEY BEGAN A SHARED CONCERT TOUR.

left Newport a star,' Robert Shelton wrote.

Dylan's association with Baez developed into something more than admiration. By August he was guesting at her concerts, and they had become lovers. In September, a few days after they had both sung to 400,000 people at the March on Washington, he moved into Baez's house in Carmel Valley, California. Musically, it was hardly a distinguished collaboration. In the early days, Baez's very straight readings of Dylan's songs undoubtedly made them palatable to a wider audience, but when they sang together her poised, full-toned contralto and his catarrhal

croak simply did not blend. But audiences loved them for their obvious empathy, and for what they seemed to represent: a union of complicated but attractive personal characteristics – her purity and strength, his eloquence and elusiveness – overlaid with the entire gamut of anti-establishment political attitudes.

The backlash was inevitable. It came in October, with an article in *Newsweek* that accused Dylan of falsifying his life story and of stealing his material ('Blowin' in the Wind' was said to have been sold to Dylan by a New Jersey high-school student). Other publications were beginning to caricature his attitudes.

Baez's straightforward view of her responsibilities as a politically aware artist soon clashed with his. For Dylan, nothing could be that simple. When, in December, three weeks after President Kennedy's assassination, the Emergency Civil Liberties Committee gave him the Tom Paine Award for epitomizing the fight for freedom and equality, he responded with a drunken acceptance speech in which he seemed to identify himself with some of Lee Harvey Oswald's supposed grievances. In a subsequent letter of apology to the committee, and in another open letter to *Broadside*, he appeared to be making the

first efforts to cut his links with organized political movements.

No such sentiments were evident in the material for his third album, which he had already begun at Columbia's studios, with Tom Wilson now firmly ensconced in the producer's chair. From its highly explicit title song onwards, *The Times They Are A-Changin'* was the apotheosis of the protest song. 'The Ballad of Hollis Brown', 'With God on Our Side', 'The Lonesome Death of Hattie Carroll' and 'Only a Pawn in Their Game' confronted specific issues without equivocation, complemented by the gentler qualities of 'Boots of Spanish Leather' – a pretty reworking of 'Girl from the North Country', written in two 'voices', with Suze in mind – and 'One Too Many Mornings', an exhausted goodbye note. In 'North Country Blues' he made an

BY THE END OF 1963, DYLAN WAS THE MOST TALKED-ABOUT YOUNG SINGER IN AMERICA, BUT THE PRESSURE WAS MAKING ITSELF FELT. HE WAS PARTICULARLY INFURIATED WHEN *NEWSWEEK* RAN A STORY ACCUSING HIM OF LYING ABOUT HIS MIDDLE-CLASS ORIGINS AND SUGGESTING THAT HE HAD BOUGHT 'BLOWIN' IN THE WIND', HIS MOST FAMOUS COMPOSITION, FROM ANOTHER SONGWRITER.

57

affecting return to the Iron Range, using his mastery of traditional techniques in a convincing portrayal of the plight of a miner's wife. But it was in the week of the *Newsweek* story that he wrote and recorded the album's closing track, 'Restless Farewell', with its seething final verse: 'Oh a false clock tries to tick out my time/To disgrace, distract and bother me/And the dirt of gossip blows into my face/And the dust of rumours covers me . . .' Life, we can assume, was getting uncomfortable.

The album was released in January 1964, with a striking image on the cover: a grainy black-and-white portrait of a twenty-two-year-old boy who looked, if anything, an old forty-two, with experience and scepticism in his downturned eyes. Just as much of an image-building exercise as the *Freewheelin'* cover, Barry Feinstein's tightly cropped *Times* photograph created the image of the archetypal protest singer. The song titles were printed beneath the title, adding to the impression of seriousness and substance.

On 3 February 1964, barely two weeks later, Dylan set out with three friends, Victor Maimudes, Paul Clayton and Pete Karman, on the journey to which he had often laid claim: into the heart of America. For a month they

wandered, their only co-ordinates a handful of Dylan concerts in Atlanta, Jackson, Denver, Berkeley and Santa Monica. They met striking miners in Kentucky, visited the writer Carl Sandburg in North Carolina, and lost themselves in the hedonistic mayhem of the New Orleans Mardi Gras. When Dylan returned to New York at the beginning of March, it was to find that his relationship with Suze, held for several months uneasily in

parallel with his affair with Baez, was over.

In May he was back in London, for a concert at the Royal Festival Hall – a prestige venue holding almost 3,000 people. This was his first exposure to the kind of hysteria that was coming. England was in the grip of a mania for the Beatles, the Rolling Stones, the Kinks, the Hollies, and a thousand other new groups who had swept away the old hierarchy of Tin

IN MAY 1964 HE ARRIVED AT HEATHROW AIRPORT FOR A CONCERT AT LONDON'S FESTIVAL HALL. AS HE TALKED TO REPORTERS, BESEECHING NOTES FROM ENGLISH FANS LAY ON THE TABLE.

DYLAN'S AUDIENCE AT THE LONDON CONCERT INCLUDED MANY MEMBERS OF THE ROCK ARISTOCRACY, WHO RECOGNIZED HIM AS THE NEW PACESETTER. HIS CORDUROY CAP, HIS JEANS AND HIS MATELOT SHIRT BECAME STAPLES OF THE SIXTIES WARDROBE.

voice of his generation's political consciousness, his new album was full of personal songs – and even incorporated a song unmistakably disavowing his former stance, which included the line: 'Lies that life is black and white spoke from my skull . . .' And he could hardly have put it more plainly than he did in 'My Back Pages', with its famous revisionist incantation: 'Ah, but I was so much older then, I'm younger than that now'.

The album moved off into an interior landscape in which murdered black servants, wicked arms dealers, assassinated presidents and starving miners were nowhere to be found. Most of the songs examined complicated relationships with women, although in 'It Ain't Me, Babe' he proved his ability to couch such sentiments in a song with a very broad appeal. This was the kind of thing that by now had other artists pestering his publishing company for advance demo tapes.

The album's centrepiece was 'Chimes of Freedom', a majestic tapestry of fractured images glimpsed on a 'wild cathedral evening' in the heart of America as he rode with Maimudes, Clayton and Karman. For those who wanted to find it, here was a reaffirmation that Bob Dylan was still interested in the human condition, although he

Pan Alley. Now their fans queued for Dylan, too, and they were the kind of fans he wanted. He saw their clothes, their hair, their style, and found himself responding to them as much as they responded to him.

In these weeks, and particularly during a short holiday in Greece, he wrote the fifteen songs that were recorded in a single day at the Columbia studios in June;

eleven of them were released in August as his fourth album, *Another Side of Bob Dylan.* 'Tom Wilson titled it that,' he said. 'I begged and pleaded with him not to do it. You know, I thought it was overstating the obvious . . . It seemed like a negation of the past, which in no way was true.' The fact was, though, that at the very moment when Bob Dylan was beginning to receive acclamation as the

wasn't going to express it through tales in 'black and white'. It also contained a song that turned out to be his first serious misjudgement, although it hardly sounded like that at the time. 'Ballad in Plain D' was a bitter, vengeful song, clearly excoriating Suze's mother and her older sister, Carla, for their part in the break-up and describing the climactic row that had ended in a scuffle between Dylan and Carla. 'That song just went too

ROBERT SHELTON (LEFT) WROTE THE PERCEPTIVE *NEW YORK TIMES* REVIEW THAT EFFECTIVELY LAUNCHED DYLAN'S CAREER. THEY REMAINED FRIENDS. HERE THEY ARE TOGETHER, ALMOST THREE YEARS LATER, BACKSTAGE AT THE 1964 NEWPORT FOLK FESTIVAL.

DYLAN WAS MOVING AWAY FROM THE PURIST FOLK SCENE. AT NEWPORT HE COULD NOT RECREATE THE PREVIOUS YEAR'S TRIUMPH. SONGS LIKE 'MR TAMBOURINE MAN' AND 'ALL I REALLY WANT TO DO' SEEMED TO BE AIMED AT ANOTHER AUDIENCE ALTOGETHER.

far,' Suze said later. Dylan eventually agreed: 'It was a mistake to record it, and I regret it.'

There was dissatisfaction in July at the Newport Folk Festival when he declined to play any of the old finger-pointing songs, giving instead a stoned and faltering performance of new material. As a direct result, Irwin Silber, the editor of *Sing Out!*, addressed an open letter to him: 'The paraphernalia of fame is getting in your way . . .'

Dylan retreated to Grossman's big house in Woodstock, an artists' community in upstate New York. In August he made a special trip back to the city to meet the Beatles, and returned again for a Hallowe'en concert at Philharmonic Hall in which his spirits seemed fully restored. Some of the older protest songs were rehabilitated, alongside two stunning new songs: 'Gates of Eden', in which his imagery reached a new peak of exotic richness, and 'It's Alright, Ma', in which he again targeted specific ills of society, but now linking a much surer poetic reach to the kind of passion he once brought to 'See That My Grave Is Kept Clean'. It was a better end than he might have expected to a year in which his growing popularity had been consistently undercut by disturbing intimations of mortality.

BY 1964, HE WAS SPENDING LESS TIME IN NEW YORK AND MORE IN WOODSTOCK, THE RUSTIC ARTISTS' COMMUNITY WHERE HE COULD WRITE IN PEACE AND RIDE HIS NEW TRIUMPH 500 AROUND THE QUIET BACK ROADS.

3. ghosts of electricity

'That thin, that

wild mercury

sound...

metallic and

bright gold'

Dylan had spent most of the autumn of 1965 at Albert Grossman's house at Bearsville in Woodstock. He still had his own apartment on West 4th Street, and he and Bobby Neuwirth occasionally made forays into the downtown night-life, but he needed to get away from the narrow Village scene. Woodstock was a pretty town with a relaxed atmosphere. He kept a motorbike in Grossman's garage, played chess at the Café Espresso, and wrote a bunch of songs that would kick-start the next big change in rock and roll.

Dylan's influence had already extended far beyond his would-be imitators on the folk scene. In Britain, the Animals, a raw Newcastle rhythm-and-blues group, had

LATE IN 1964, DYLAN AND HIS FAITHFUL COMPANION VICTOR MAIMUDES AT ALBERT AND SALLY GROSSMAN'S MANSION IN BEARSVILLE, JUST OUTSIDE WOODSTOCK. A SIGN AT THE ENTRANCE TO THE DRIVEWAY READ 'IF YOU HAVE NOT TELEPHONED, YOU ARE TRESPASSING'.

been in the charts with dense, powerful versions of 'Baby Let Me Follow You Down' (retitled 'Baby Let Me Take You Home') and 'House of the Rising Sun', both inspired by Dylan's first album.

John Lennon, too, had played Dylan's records ceaselessly; when they met in August 1964, during the Beatles' triumphant second US tour, Dylan rolled the Liverpool group's first joints in a New York hotel room. And in December, when the *Beatles for Sale* album was released in Britain, Dylan's influence could clearly be heard in Lennon's 'I'm a Loser', the American's folkish cadences and his nonconformist attitude modifying the style of a young Englishman raised on Presley and Motown. It would be exaggerating the case to say that Dylan turned the Beatles from mop-tops to hop-heads, but he was certainly a liberating influence on Lennon, feeding the natural anti-establishment truculence that increasingly defined the group's direction. 'You've Got to Hide Your Love Away', (released on the soundtrack of *Help!* in the summer of 1965) found Lennon playing a straightforward homage; with *Rubber Soul* 's 'Norwegian Wood' at the end of the year Lennon was to prove that he could make something original of his Dylan fixation.

Dylan's image was now taking on a life of its own: to the public, the press and some of his peers, he had become a strange, exotic creature with the characteristics of a Messiah or an oracle. He was also slipping into the patterns of a new social life. Drinking in the Kettle of Fish (a MacDougal Street bar) with Neuwirth just before Christmas, he met Edie Sedgwick, a young model from an old Massachusetts family who was spending her time running from one discotheque to another. An exquisite creature with a mesmerizingly androgynous face, the perfect cross between a debutante and a street kid, the twenty-two-year-old Sedgwick was only a few weeks away from meeting Andy Warhol and becoming part of the crowd of 'superstars' who hung around the pop artist's silver-foil-lined studio, the Factory. She was different from the long-haired girls who sat hypnotized at Dylan's feet as he sang twenty-verse traditional ballads in folk clubs. So was another woman he'd just met: Sara Lowndes, a friend of Sally Grossman (his manager's wife), and a regular guest at the Bearsville estate. A dark, quiet, serene beauty – the ex-wife of a senior executive of Hugh Hefner's Playboy empire – Sara was at the other end of the scale from the talkative, socially hyperactive and, as it

turned out, hugely vulnerable Edie.

As he prepared to record his fifth album in New York in mid-January 1965, Dylan drew from all this the strength to push through a major change of style, taking particular encouragement from the way the new English beat groups seemed unafraid to experiment. They'd connected with the audience he was after in just the way he wanted to, blending the content of the folk-based music with the electricity of rock and roll. Moreover, they seemed to be able to pull it off without having to apologize to anyone, without caring what Midwestern disc jockeys or the record company's accountants had to say.

On 14 January, he gave it a shot. Waiting for him in Columbia's Studio A that day were two electric guitarists, Al Gorgoni and Kenny Rankin; pianists Paul Griffin and Frank Owens; John Sebastian (later to lead the Lovin' Spoonful) on bass guitar; and Bobby Gregg at the drums. Tom Wilson had not chosen young tearaways; these were seasoned session men. But they were younger and more responsive than the jazz musicians John Hammond had provided for 'Mixed-Up Confusion', and the results were very different.

Dylan had brought with him a song called 'Subterranean

65

THE JANUARY 1965 SESSIONS FOR *BRINGING IT ALL BACK HOME* REPRESENTED A SIGNIFICANT BREAK FROM THE FORMAT OF THE FIRST FOUR ALBUMS, WITH A RHYTHM SECTION ADDED IN AN ATTEMPT TO INJECT THE ENERGY OF ROCK AND ROLL INTO DYLAN'S COMPLEX SONGS.

ALTHOUGH IT BEGAN WITH THE RACKETY ELECTRIC BLUES OF 'SUBTERRANEAN HOMESICK BLUES', HALF THE NEW ALBUM WAS NEVERTHELESS MADE UP OF ACOUSTIC SONGS.

Homesick Blues', a kind of absurdist transformation of Chuck Berry's 'Too Much Monkey Business', itself a classic of rapid-fire rock-and-roll wordplay. We now know that at first he ran it through in a solo acoustic version, but within minutes he had the rhythm section playing along in an engaging, ramshackle kind of jam that didn't really have any precedent in the ten-year history of rock. Dylan was throwing the music together, and that was how it sounded. The spontaneity led to rough edges, and he made sure that they weren't smoothed over. He wasn't after any sort of polish: he wanted spirit and decibels, an unholy racket. That was what he got in this and the five other songs – 'Maggie's Farm', 'On the Road Again', 'Outlaw Blues', 'Bob Dylan's 115th Dream' and 'If You Gotta Go, Go Now' – recorded by that line-up. It was a lurching, formless, honky-tonk kind of noise, curiously lacking in style, which made the English rock groups – even the Yardbirds or the Kinks – sound polished by comparison; but it did make a good foil for his voice, which for the first time seemed to be that of a young man.

The next day, when Dylan recorded the balance of the album, the mood was different. Now he turned to three songs that he'd already tried out at his summer and autumn concerts. 'Mr Tambourine Man', 'It's Alright, Ma (I'm Only Bleeding)' and 'Gates of Eden' took the complexities of 'Hard Rain' and 'Chimes of Freedom' a step further. In these songs, Dylan showed how he could construct a lyric that would make his listeners word-giddy, connecting images that might make no literal sense but somehow evoked a stronger response than ever. With 'Mr Tambourine Man' and 'Gates of Eden' especially, he seemed to be inviting comparisons with everyone from the authors of the Old Testament through mediaeval troubadours and William Blake to Apollinaire and Rimbaud. The effect was dazzling and disturbing: who knew what the 'four-legged forest clouds' were, upon which the cowboy angel rode? Why did the lamppost stand with folded arms? What exactly did the motorcycle

In Columbia's Studio A on 15 January, 1965. Left to right: journalist Al Aronowitz, producer Tom Wilson, unidentified musician, Dylan, and manager Albert Grossman.

black madonna two-wheeled gypsy queen have against the grey-flannel dwarf? But, since every word carried such dark and strange passion that it seemed to have been burnt into the vinyl, who cared? His audience was very ready for him. It is easy to say that adolescent immaturity made them susceptible to his pretension, but that isn't really true. Twenty-five years later, it remains possible to enjoy these songs simply for the sound the words make, for the fleeting visions they bring into being, and for the occasional phrase so original and razor-sharp that it has entered the language.

By contrast, 'It's Alright, Ma' dazzled in the opposite way – an observation of contemporary life so sweeping in its scope yet so specific and implacable in its judgements that it could stand as a permanent summary of his world-view. Railing against politicians, advertising men, educators, preachers, lawyers and yes-men great or small, its narrator seemed precariously balanced on the edge of his own sanity, fighting to keep the truth in view. The blizzard of indictments came with a literally monotonous non-melody, all the musical movement provided by a descending guitar pattern grown from the seed of 'See that My Grave Is Kept Clean'.

Dylan's voice, never varying from a sort of morbid blankness, played against the urgency of the guitar to great dramatic effect, enhanced by the sudden lone harmonica blast punctuating each chorus.

These three songs were recorded on 15 January in simple acoustic style (with the discreet Bruce Langhorne adding graceful guitar fills to 'Mr Tambourine Man'). In fact, they are said by a witness to have been recorded in a single sweep, one after another, without pauses for playbacks – a remarkable enough feat, given their length and complexity, but made quite astonishing by the controlled intensity of Dylan's delivery. On a fourth song, 'It's All Over Now, Baby Blue', Bill Lee played string bass. For 'She Belongs to Me' and 'Love Minus Zero/No Limit', Langhorne and Lee were joined by John Hammond Jr's acoustic guitar and Bobby Gregg's unobtrusive drums. All these songs, unified by their reflective quality, sounded as though they'd been conceived as acoustic solo pieces, and could easily be performed by Dylan on his own in concert.

The album's title, *Bringing It All Back Home*, could be taken both ways. Old folkies might see within it an affirmation of what they imagined to be his roots – in Woody Guthrie and Muddy

In New York on 15 January 1965, in one unbroken sequence, he recorded 'Mr Tambourine Man', 'It's Alright, Ma (I'm Only Bleeding)' and 'Gates of Eden', three of his richest and most complex acoustic songs. The critic Paul Williams called it 'easily the greatest breath drawn by an American artist since Ginsberg and Kerouac exhaled *Howl* and *On the Road* a decade earlier'.

© 1965 FRED W. MCDARRAH

CONFIDENCE RAN HIGH AFTER THE COMPLETION OF THE NEW ALBUM AND ITS RELEASE A BARE NINE WEEKS LATER. HERE HE IS IN NEW YORK'S SHERIDAN SQUARE ON 22 JANUARY 1965, WITH *BRINGING IT ALL BACK HOME* SAFELY IN THE CAN.

Waters. The hip young audience could put it together with the rock-and-roll stylings and infer that here was where Dylan's head had really been all the time. If he'd wanted to lead his old fans gently into his new music, the album would have begun with 'It's Alright, Ma', or maybe 'She Belongs to Me'. The fact that he put 'Subterranean Homesick Blues' at the top of the running order meant only one thing: he was prepared to lose those people, if he had to.

The cover image certainly indicated that he was telling a different story: no more dust-bowl balladeer poses, no more waif on a snowbound 4th Street. Here, in a composition artfully arranged by the

photographer Daniel Kramer, Dylan poses — immaculately glamorous in dark jacket, striped tab-collar shirt and ornate cuff links, his hair styled into a luxurious bouffant, cradling a cold-eyed, smoke-haired kitten — in a room of his manager's house, the sleek Sally Grossman lounging behind him in a scarlet trouser-suit like a figure from a society magazine. Around them, on the velvet *chaise-longue* and the Regency mantelpiece, are arrayed books and magazines and album covers and *objets trouvés*: a fall-out shelter sign; a *Time* magazine with Lyndon Johnson on the cover; albums by Lotte Lenya, Robert Johnson, Eric Von Schmidt, the

Impressions and Dylan himself; a glass mosaic image of a sad clown's face made by the singer as a gift for the Café Espresso's proprietor. Kramer shot the set-up through a lens that gave a fish-eye effect without distorting the perspective, lending the image a hallucinatory quality. Prepare yourself, the customer was being told, for dreams and visions.

While Dylan waited for the album's release, he went on the road. First there were a handful of American concerts with Baez (these were to be their last together). In March, *Bringing It All Back Home* was released, making its way into the US top ten. A few weeks

AFTER THE INNOCENT HOBO OF THE EARLY
ALBUM COVERS, THE PORTRAIT OF JADED
SOPHISTICATION CAPTURED BY THE
PHOTOGRAPHER DANIEL KRAMER FOR THE
JACKET OF *BRINGING IT ALL BACK HOME*,
MATCHING THE ELEGANT ENNUI OF
COMPETITORS LIKE THE ROLLING STONES,
CAME AS A DISTINCT SHOCK TO SOME OLD
FANS. THE WOMAN IS HIS MANAGER'S
WIFE, SALLY GROSSMAN.

OPPOSITE: JOAN BAEZ CAME TO BRITAIN WITH HIM BUT — TO HER SURPRISE — SHE WAS NOT INVITED ON STAGE, AND FOUND HERSELF FROZEN OUT OF THE DRESSING ROOM CAMARADERIE ESTABLISHED BY DYLAN AND HIS NEW TRAVELLING COMPANION, THE SINGER–PAINTER BOBBY NEUWIRTH. 'I RODE ON HER,' DYLAN WAS TO SAY, 'BUT I DON'T THINK I OWE HER ANYTHING.'

DYLANMANIA: WHEN HE ARRIVED AT HEATHROW ON 27 APRIL 1965 FOR A SHORT BRITISH TOUR, HE FOUND ENTHUSIASM FOR THE MANIFESTATIONS OF THE SWINGING SIXTIES AT ITS HEIGHT.

MICHAEL OCHS ARCHIVES

later, 'Subterranean Homesick Blues' came out as a 45, and lines such as 'Don't follow leaders/Watch the parking meters' and 'You don't need a weatherman/To know which way the wind blows' were heard on Top 40 radio – albeit briefly, as the record rose no higher than number thirty-nine.

On 26 April Dylan left New York for a short tour of England, where hysteria was building. Britain is a small island: news travels fast, crazes catch on quickly, and the attention span is short. At this point, early in 1965, Swinging London was reaching its peak, the search for novelty was a national occupation, and the news editors of national newspapers were under orders to get the new youth culture into their pages. Their response, usually, was to send out middle-aged reporters whose knowledge of the pop scene was limited to watching aghast as their mod offspring experimented with free love, soft drugs and the new peacock fashions from Carnaby Street. To them, Dylan sounded like good copy: they saw a pop singer who wasn't cute like the Beatles, whose songs amounted to a blanket condemnation of the social and political system, and who nevertheless exerted some strange hold over their fifteen-year-old daughters. Reducing him to the language of headlines, they saw him as the equivalent of the Marlon Brando figure in *The Wild One*: 'What're you rebelling against, Johnny?' 'What you've got?' They could get a story out of this one.

The media's efforts are preserved in *Don't Look Back*, the ninety-minute documentary film of the tour made for Dylan and Grossman by D.A. Pennebaker, a young director who'd been recommended by Sara Lowndes. Almost nobody came out of this extraordinary piece of *cinéma vérité* with their reputation intact: not the scheming Grossman, heard playing greasy games in negotiation with TV companies and being unbelievably rude to a hotel bellboy; not Bobby Neuwirth, Dylan's accomplice,

The English singer Dana Gillespie was among those with whom he spent time on the 1965 tour.

smirking behind his matching shades; not Baez, embarrassingly unaware that her relationship with Dylan was well past its sell-by date — unlike the viewer, who can see it in Dylan's complete indifference to her (he'd rather be larking with Neuwirth), or Pennebaker, whose last shot of her is an exit from the dressing room, closing the door behind her; not Alan Price, the Animals' organist, swilling vodka and orange from individual bottles in a drunken backstage stupor; not the smug, flaccid Donovan; and, in particular, not the entire cast of the British press — from the hard-bitten reporter who greeted him at the airport with an incisive 'How long is it since you've been here?' to the boy from a student newspaper who unwisely attempted to engage him in a dialogue on the meaning of existence and was slowly taken apart.

By this time, Dylan had been asked so many stupid questions that he was the master of every exchange. Observing him dealing with his inquisitors — from the naïve through the aggressive to the sycophantic — was like watching an expert fencer faced with a blindfolded man wearing boxing gloves. His mind only half on the job, Dylan nicked and slashed and cut strips off the reporters where and when he chose,

performing the task so deftly that they often didn't even notice until they were out of the room. His sympathy was reserved for non-professionals: a gaggle of sweetly besotted Liverpool schoolgirls wanting his autograph, four young beat musicians paying honest homage, even the gushing High Sheriff's Lady in Newcastle with her mortified teenage sons shuffling in the background. You could only like the Bob Dylan of *Don't Look Back* as a human being if you could imagine the phenomenal pressure put on his patience and his imagination by a life in which every working day was filled with such demands. Imagine being Bob Dylan in a world in which every stranger seemed to have his own idea of who Bob Dylan was.

Maybe the tension in the film can be explained by the fact that the Bob Dylan who took the stage at Sheffield City Hall on 30 April 1965 for the tour's first concert was not the Bob Dylan of 14 January in Columbia's Studio A. Committed to a tour booked the previous year, facing an audience dying to hear 'The Times They Are A-Changin' ' (which had been in the British singles charts only a month before) and 'Blowin' in the Wind', he had to turn himself back into something he no longer wanted to be. The performances were mixed: the older songs, notably 'Times They Are A-Changin' ', were given a rushed, perfunctory treatment, while the newer ones, particularly 'It's Alright, Ma' and 'Gates of Eden', clearly engaged more of his attention. His own mood probably wasn't helped by the atmosphere of hushed reverence. His arrival on stage was greeted with loud applause, as was the end of each song, but while he changed harmonicas or took a drink of water from the glass on his high stool there was a rapt silence as the audience inspected this young legend moving and breathing. Any attempt on his part at making a joke between songs resulted only in a nervous tittering. It must have been unnerving enough to make him wish that he'd had other musicians on stage to divert some of the attention.

The exception to this reaction was the first concert at the Royal Albert Hall. The film shows Dylan clearly apprehensive both of the auditorium – in terms of prestige, the English equivalent of Carnegie Hall – and of the audience, which numbered the entire dramatis personae of fashionable London. The significance of the occasion was as obvious to him then as it is to us now. Afterwards, as he came down the stairs into the dressing room, gulping for air, the waves of applause continued to echo. 'Actually,' he said to Neuwirth, looking for a smart, dismissive remark to keep the shield up, 'applause is kinda bullshit . . .' And a moment later, collecting himself: 'I feel like I've been through some kinda thing, man . . . something special about that.'

The Bob Dylan he wanted to be appeared once or twice in *Don't Look Back*, notably when he was alone with a piano in the dressing room, testing a chord sequence that sounded like a variation on one of rock and roll's most hallowed formulas: the I-IV-V progression which had been the foundation of Ritchie Valens's 'La Bamba', of the Isley Brothers' 'Twist and Shout', and of the Kingsmen's 'Louie Louie'. By the time he got back to America, he was ready to turn this little three-chord trick into a song which, more than any other, would signify the change he was going through.

First he was given another shove by the appearance in the US singles charts of 'Mr Tambourine Man', the first release by a Los Angeles quintet called the Byrds, a bunch of young folk musicians who'd heard the Beatles, got hold of a publisher's acetate of *Bringing It All Back Home*, and

RONALD GRANT ARCHIVE

THE BRITISH TOUR WAS IMMORTALIZED IN D.A. PENNEBAKER'S *DON'T LOOK BACK*, AN UTTERLY UNVARNISHED PORTRAIT OF BACKSTAGE LIFE EMBARRASSING TO ALMOST EVERYONE CONCERNED — NOT LEAST ALAN PRICE OF THE ANIMALS, WHOSE PROPS WERE A PIANO AND A BOTTLE OF VODKA.

THE BYRDS' CHART-TOPPING VERSION OF 'MR TAMBOURINE MAN' MADE ELECTRIC FOLK-ROCK THE SOUND OF 1965. HERE DYLAN GUESTS WITH THEM AT CIRO'S, THE HOLLYWOOD NIGHT CLUB THAT WAS THEIR BASE.

made the brilliant decision to create a rock and roll version of one of its longest and most complicated songs. The silvery electric arpeggios of Jim McGuinn's electric twelve-string guitar were the key, echoing the 'jingle-jangle morning' of the song's chorus and bringing the strumming and finger-picking of folk guitar into the world that the 1965 pop-music audience inhabited. In a mere two and a quarter minutes, they could reflect only a fraction of the substance of Dylan's original version, but the strength of the arrangement, and the jangling-into-infinity fade-out in particular, gave it another kind of epic grandeur. In those two and a quarter minutes, the Byrds accomplished what Dylan had not quite managed to

achieve: they had invented folk-rock.

Ironically the Byrds' producer, like Dylan's, had insisted on the use of session men to get the sound he wanted. But the Los Angeles session men chosen by Terry Melcher — rhythm guitarist/pianist Leon Russell, bass guitarist Larry Knechtel and drummer Hal Blaine — were younger than the men Dylan had been using in New York, and crazier. They were used to dealing with people like Phil Spector, who wanted a young sound, a sound that hadn't been made before. They weren't constrained by a need to obey the rules. It was a lesson that Dylan, who played with the Byrds at Ciro's (the Sunset Boulevard club where they'd been discovered), took to heart — the more so as their success soon led to a string of copies. The Turtles recorded 'It Ain't Me, Babe', Manfred Mann had an English hit with 'If You Gotta Go, Go Now', Cher released a Byrds-cum-Spector version of 'All I Really Want to Do', and the rejected Baez herself released 'It's All Over Now, Baby Blue' (a song that may itself have been generated in part by the ending of their affair).

Others tried to write their own Bob Dylan songs, like Sonny Bono with 'Laugh at Me', Buffy Sainte-Marie with 'The Universal Soldier' and, of

course, Donovan with 'Catch the Wind'. Back in Hollywood, the canny young publisher Lou Adler gave his staff songwriter P.F. Sloan an acoustic guitar and a Bob Dylan cap, locked him in a Hollywood hotel room for a weekend, and was greeted on the Monday morning with a batch of ready-made folk-rock protest songs, including the hilariously overblown 'Eve of Destruction', which became a worldwide number one for an ex-New Christy Minstrel named Barry McGuire, and 'Sins of the Family', which didn't have quite the same magical effect on Sloan's own singing career.

In June 1965, while the Byrds made their unstoppable ascent to the number one position in the American and British singles charts, Dylan went back into the Columbia studios. There, on 15 June, he did something unusual: the man who until now had been noted for his relaxed approach to studio recording, who seldom went for more than two or three takes on any song, devoted most of an entire session to a single piece.

The song in question had its seed in the little chord sequence tried on the backstage piano in England. It had been completed in a Woodstock cabin that he was sharing with Sara Lowndes, who — despite other dalliances

— was emerging as a significant factor in his life. Now the song had grown into something with four verses and a majestic chorus. 'Like a Rolling Stone' was its name, and at first Dylan and Wilson couldn't decide how to record it.

The holdovers from the previous session were Bobby Gregg and Paul Griffin. There was a new bass guitarist, Harvey Brooks. Also in the studio that day were a pair of younger men. The first was Mike Bloomfield, a twenty-year-old prodigy from Chicago who played lead guitar with the Paul Butterfield Blues Band. Dylan had met Bloomfield at a Chicago club two years earlier; now he'd heard him playing full-tilt blues with Butterfield, whose back-to-the-roots philosophy had been made plain on the band's first album for Elektra, recorded in New York at the beginning of the year. Bloomfield idolized people like Buddy Guy and Albert King, and had no inhibitions about putting loud blues-rock licks behind Dylan's songs. The second of the younger musicians was Al Kooper, a twenty-one-year-old New Yorker who'd been in and out of groups from the age of fifteen and had written 'This Diamond Ring', a number one single for Gary Lewis and the Playboys that January. Kooper, who played guitar and piano,

had been invited along by Tom Wilson, but his function was unclear as the session began.

According to Dylan, the lyric of 'Like a Rolling Stone' had emerged from ten pages of 'vomitic' writing. In the process, it had been distilled to perfection. Its venomous sarcasm, directed at a girl who may have been in part the poor little rich girl Edie Sedgwick, was unprecedented. The gallery of Fellini-esque secondary characters — the mystery tramp, the clowns and jugglers, the diplomat, Napoleon in rags — were no longer the point of the song, but populated instead a severely personal attack.

Dylan began at the piano, running through a version of the song in waltz time,

BY MID-1965, DYLAN WAS WRITING MORE AND MORE SONGS AT THE PIANO. 'LIKE A ROLLING STONE' BEGAN AS A VARIATION ON THE SIMPLE THREE-CHORD PATTERN OF 'LA BAMBA' AND 'LOUIE LOUIE', BECAME A STATELY MINUET, AND FINISHED UP ON 15 JUNE 1965 IN COLUMBIA'S STUDIO A AS A FULLY-FLEDGED MASTERPIECE..

Bloomfield joining in tentatively and the others listening to pick up the structure. Gradually it took shape, with Gregg and Brooks slipping from the original lumpy, lurching gait into a calm, majestic 4/4, Griffin adding barrelhouse fills, Bloomfield anchoring the whole thing with ringing Telecaster flourishes. Finally, Dylan made the crucial decision. What he wanted, he said, was an organ to go with the piano. Al Kooper, sitting around unemployed during the run-throughs, was pressed into service by Wilson. He'd never played an organ before, but the studio's Hammond B3 was set to the sound they wanted and he started to play a simple line, doing little more than punching out simple chords in the upper register, the whirling Leslie speaker making the notes hang and shiver in the air. Right there, Dylan heard what he'd been looking for. He stopped the take, and asked Wilson to turn the organ up. The next take was it. After Gregg's opening snare-drum shot, the first sound you hear is that of Kooper holding his shivering, silvery note.

At six and a quarter minutes, 'Like a Rolling Stone' was twice the length that pop singles were supposed to be, and yet it seemed to carry not an ounce of superfluous

weight. It sounds simple now, just seven instruments recorded live in a studio without any trickery, but on a first hearing its massiveness was what made the impact: it seemed like some great baroque cathedral of sound, a giant structure hung with all kinds of exotic decoration. A month later it was in the shops, on the radio, heading into history as a statement: Bob Dylan had finally discovered the way his music should sound. It became his first million-selling single and inspired his contemporaries to exert themselves in an effort to make ever more epic use of the 45rpm seven-inch format. The Beach Boys' 'Good Vibrations', the Beatles' 'Strawberry Fields Forever' and the Four Tops' 'Reach Out, I'll Be There' could not have existed had 'Like a Rolling Stone' not redefined the limits of their ambition.

At this stage, and somewhat mystifyingly, considering the success of the 'Rolling Stone' session, Dylan decided to change producers again. Tom Wilson was out, replaced by Bob Johnston, a young CBS staff producer who came from Nashville and who had produced a variety of the label's artists, including Louis Armstrong and Aretha Franklin. Using the same musicians, over the next six weeks Dylan recorded enough

material to fill out an LP. The combination of Bloomfield's wild, screaming guitar and Kooper's wailing Hammond defined the new sound on songs like 'Tombstone Blues' and 'From a Buick 6'; a subtler key texture was the blend of organ and piano, a staple of gospel music but hardly heard before in pop. As a result, the gentler songs, such as 'Queen Jane Approximately' and 'Just Like Tom Thumb's Blues', had a sumptuousness that was almost decadent. The content of these songs also fuelled the growing habit of paying unusually close attention to Dylan's words. 'Desolation Row' (recorded with just two acoustic guitars and a string bass) took the strain of surrealistic ballads that had begun with 'Chimes of Freedom' to a new level. Here was the modern world's own 'Waste Land', the deeply encoded psychogram of a generation.

As usual, the audiences at Dylan's concerts had different expectations from the admirers who bought his records after hearing them on the radio. At the end of July, with 'Like a Rolling Stone' in the charts and the new album, *Highway 61 Revisited*, almost completed, he was due to make his third consecutive appearance at the Newport Folk Festival, where his unofficial coronation had taken

THE 1965 NEWPORT FESTIVAL PRODUCED ANOTHER TURNING POINT. FIRST, THOUGH, DYLAN TRIED TO SATISFY HIS OLD AUDIENCE BY SINGING 'MR TAMBOURINE MAN' AND 'ALL I REALLY WANT TO DO' AT A WORKSHOP SESSION ON THE AFTERNOON OF 24 JULY.

TWENTY-FOUR HOURS AFTER THE WORKSHOP PERFORMANCE, HE WAS TRANSFORMED INTO THE AVENGING ANGEL OF ROCK AND ROLL: PALE GREEN POLKA- DOT SHIRT, TIGHT BLACK TROUSERS, CUBAN-HEELED BOOTS, RAY-BANS, HAIR LIKE SOLID SMOKE, READY TO RAISE A NEAR-RIOT IN FREEBODY PARK.

place in 1963. Again, the Bob Dylan of Daniel Kramer's *Highway 61* cover shot, in his vaguely proto-psychedelic shirt and Triumph motorcycle T-shirt, was not the Bob Dylan of the Newport audience's imagination. No one seems quite sure how it came about, of the degree of pre-planning involved, but what happened was that Dylan played a set with the Paul Butterfield Blues Band, and caused a riot.

That the Butterfield Band was playing at Newport at all had led to a row within the festival's board of directors, but it was nothing compared with what happened when on the event's penultimate day Dylan turned up with Kooper and Neuwirth, looking like a bunch of dandy English rock stars in their puffed-sleeve shirts and big sunglasses. Dylan had probably already decided that he wanted to use the band rather than make his scheduled solo appearance, and so, with Kooper added on organ and Barry Goldberg on piano, they stayed up all night rehearsing in one of the big old Newport mansions near the festival compound. The next day, Dylan was due to play in the evening. Within seconds of the music beginning, there was pandemonium: the hard electric sound of 'Maggie's Farm' brought booing from the traditionalists in the audience and created a ferocious argument backstage, where Alan Lomax and Pete Seeger

CURIOUSLY UNHASSLED IN THE ARTISTS'
BACKSTAGE COMPOUND, HE AND ALBERT
GROSSMAN PLOT THE EVENING'S SURPRISE.

NEWPORT FOLK FESTIVAL

DYLAN'S BAND AT NEWPORT FEATURED THE GUITARIST MIKE BLOOMFIELD AND THE BASS-GUITARIST JEROME ARNOLD (BOTH OF THE PAUL BUTTERFIELD BLUES BAND) AND THE ORGANIST AL KOOPER. UNSEEN ARE THE PIANIST BARRY GOLDBERG AND A THIRD BUTTERFIELD MUSICIAN, THE DRUMMER SAMMY LAY. FOR THE FIRST TIME IN PUBLIC, DYLAN HAS PUT ASIDE HIS ACOUSTIC JUMBO GUITAR FOR A MEAN BLACK FENDER STRATOCASTER.

were among the distinguished board members trying desperately to find someone to turn the racket down. As the musicians careered on through 'Like a Rolling Stone' and a prototype of 'It Takes a Lot to Laugh, It Takes a Train to Cry' with more energy and volume than actual synchronization, Dylan may have flashed back eight years, to Hibbing High School's annual talent contest, when the principal got the janitor to cut the power on his little amateur band.

Witnesses at Newport say

that he was quite badly shaken by the vehemence of the response, and after the band's set, which lasted only three songs (less than twenty-five minutes in all), he agreed to calm the place down by playing two acoustic numbers, 'It's All Over Now, Baby Blue' and 'Mr Tambourine Man'. And with that, he said farewell to the folk scene which had first nourished his talent and then done its level best to throttle him.

Dylan tore back to New York and spat out the last few songs for *Highway 61 Revisited* in less than a week; one of them, 'Ballad of a Thin Man', was specifically addressed to his critics. Its derisive chorus – 'Something is happening here, and you don't know what it is/Do you, Mr Jones?' – spoke for every sulky adolescent having trouble with the adult world. Dylan also added a song called 'Positively 4th Street', which would be his next single. It increased the level of personal spite beyond even 'Like a Rolling Stone', and remains the most vicious put-down song in all rock and roll. Ostensibly about a girl, it may just as easily have been another dismissive wave to his old world. 'I wish that for just one time you could stand inside my shoes/You'd know what a drag it is to see you' was the parting shot, drawled over a background that was like a copy of 'Like a Rolling Stone' etched with acid. Within weeks, both album and single were out, and snarling their way up the charts.

In between times he was working on the novel that many publishers had been urging him to write since they'd spotted his idiosyncratic biographical poetry on the back of various record jackets – *The Times They Are A-Changin'*, *Another Side*, *Bringing It All Back Home*, Peter, Paul and Mary's *In the Wind*, Baez's *In Concert Vol.2*

– and in his programme notes and open letters to *Broadside* and the Civil Liberties Committee.

He had begun working on it in a desultory way as early as 1963, assembling it on scraps of paper, disdaining from the beginning anything like a narrative structure. There were discussions with the poet Lawrence Ferlinghetti, whose San Francisco-based City Lights imprint had published Allen Ginsberg's *Howl* and other significant pieces of beat literature, but it wasn't until the establishment firm of Macmillan showed an interest in 1964 that the project took on a real life. The original idea was to accompany Dylan's text with the photographs of Barry Feinstein, the old friend who had shot the cover of *The Times They Are A-Changin'* and who was now married to Mary Travers. Then it became a text-only collage of episodes and meditations, using William Burroughs's cut-up technique, freeing the author from all responsibility for narrative or any other kind of coherence.

Grossman negotiated a deal with Macmillan, and Dylan worked on through the middle of 1965 (in *Don't Look Back*, he was seen pecking away at an old typewriter in his hotel rooms). One working title was *Bob Dylan Off the Record*; the eventual name, *Tarantula*, may have been borrowed from

Nietzsche. But there were more urgent tasks at hand, and although interviewers kept asking him about the book, he was reluctant to refer to it in any but the most oblique and unhelpful terms.

Now he needed to go on the road again, to find the audience beyond the folk festivals. Albert Grossman had booked him two big concerts: one at the Forest Hills tennis stadium in New York on 28 August, and the other at the Hollywood Bowl on 3 September. He had Kooper and a new bass guitarist, Harvey Brooks, who'd played on the *Highway 61* sessions, but he couldn't take any members of the Bloomfield Band, who were working, so he had to look elsewhere.

John Hammond Jr had been recording with a bunch of Toronto-based musicians – mostly Canadians – who, when they earned their money backing the veteran rocker Ronnie Hawkins around the clubs, called themselves the Hawks. Mary Martin, one of Grossman's assistants, was herself from Toronto and brought them to the attention of Dylan; he called up their guitarist, Jaime 'Robbie' Robertson, and asked him if he and the band's drummer, Levon Helm, would join him for the two concerts.

The new five-piece band rehearsed in New York for a couple of weeks and then assembled at Forest Hills. On a wet and windy night, in front of something like 15,000 people, Dylan played an acoustic set first, and after an intermission the whole outfit took the stage. 'Tombstone Blues' was the first song, followed by 'I Don't Believe You', 'From a Buick 6', 'Maggie's Farm', 'It Ain't Me, Babe', 'Ballad of a Thin Man' and 'Like a Rolling Stone'. Dylan had warned his new sidemen to expect a certain amount of unrest – 'Keep playing no matter how weird it gets' – but even he must have been disconcerted: the audience might as well have come direct from Newport. They booed from start to finish. Later, Kooper said sadly: 'They booed at Forest Hills because they'd read that they were supposed to.'

Depressing as this may have been, it didn't put Dylan off. He may even have found encouragement a few days later, when the Hollywood Bowl audience was slightly more appreciative, to the extent of requesting an encore. Anyway, he was already committed to begin a large-scale tour in Texas at the end of August. When Kooper, who didn't want to play to rednecks, bailed out, Robertson and Helm took the

PLANNING A JACKET PHOTOGRAPH FOR HIS NOVEL, *TARANTULA*, DYLAN AND DANIEL KRAMER RECREATED THE MOOD OF THE *BRINGING IT ALL BACK HOME* COVER, WITH SALLY GROSSMAN REPLACED BY SARA LOWNDES. BUT PUBLICATION WAS POSTPONED, AND WHEN THE NOVEL FINALLY APPEARED IN 1971 THE PICTURE WAS NOT USED.

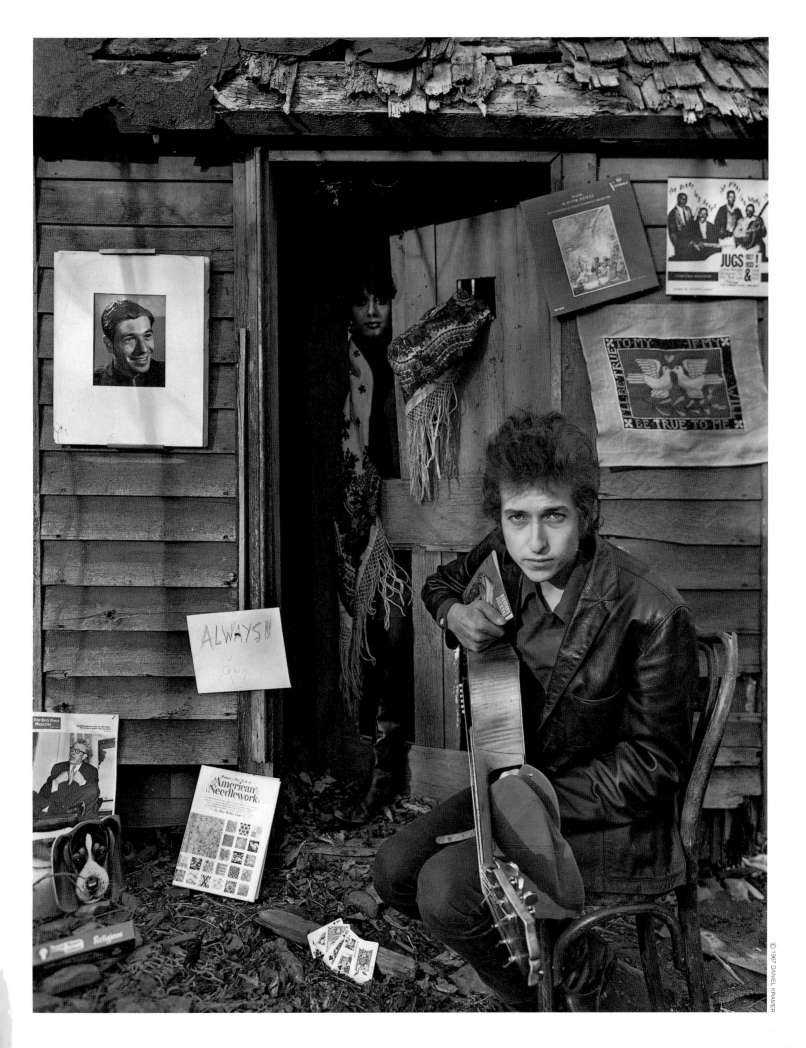

A MONTH AFTER NEWPORT, DYLAN
APPEARED WITH A NEW BAND, INCLUDING
ROBBIE ROBERTSON AND LEVON HELM OF
THE HAWKS, IN THE AMPHITHEATRE AT
FOREST HILLS IN NEW YORK, WHERE 15,000
PEOPLE GAVE A VERY MIXED RECEPTION TO
HIS ELECTRIC MUSIC. ABOVE: WORKING
ON THE SET LIST WITH AL KOOPER —
'TOMBSTONE BLUES' IN A, 'I DON'T
BELIEVE YOU' IN E, 'FROM A BUICK 6' IN A,
'LIKE A ROLLING STONE' IN THE PIANO KEY
OF C, ETC. RIGHT: MEDITATING
BACKSTAGE ON THE FIRESTORM HE IS
ABOUT TO UNLEASH.

opportunity to persuade Dylan to recruit the rest of the Hawks. So out, too, went Harvey Brooks, and in came the bass guitarist Rick Danko, the organist Garth Hudson and the pianist Richard Manuel. Their rehearsals took place in Toronto, where the Hawks were playing a club.

The Hawks were rock and roll craftsmen, and were initially suspicious of the young folk musician, whose music they hadn't heard before they played with him for the first time. 'There was a lot of strumming going on in this music,' Robbie Robertson said, remembering his reaction to folkies, 'and we didn't play with strummers.' The Hawks had honed their musicianship in countless juke joints around

America, playing rhythm and blues to the toughest audiences. To begin with, they didn't know Bob Dylan's music from a hole in the ground; what they knew about was Chuck Berry and Bo Diddley. But they were young, they were intelligent, and it didn't take them long to get the idea. Dylan gave them simple structures and plenty of room; he even turned out to be a rock and roller himself. They let him take care of the words. Robertson's guitar lashed against his voice with more discipline than Bloomfield's; Hudson and Manuel summoned up a range of rich textures with a joint understanding that went beyond anything Kooper and Griffin could manage. Danko and Helm were a finely grooved rhythm team who could put a heavy R&B kick into Dylan's songs. They were seasoned. Between them, they made the English competition sound like children playing with toys. Within a few weeks they were creating on stage every night music that struck many people as representing an absolute pinnacle of what rock and roll could be.

Not that you could tell from the way the audiences responded at the time. Dylan had now fixed on the formula of an acoustic first half followed by an electric set, and there were boos mixed with

cheers for the latter almost every night.

The tour wound across America, arriving on the East Coast at the end of November. There, on the 25th of the month, Dylan secretly married Sara Lowndes, turning up to play as scheduled in Chicago the following night. But a few days later there was a divorce: Levon Helm, discouraged by the audience response, not understanding why he should be paid to get jeered every night, quit and was replaced first by Bobby Gregg, then by Sandy Konikoff and finally by Mickey Jones. As Gregg settled in, Dylan celebrated his wedded bliss by releasing his first recording with the new line-up. The withering 'Can You Please Crawl Out Your Window' could have been labelled 'Like a Rolling Stone Pt 3'; but it seemed the audience was tiring of the formula. Despite the success of its predecessors, this release couldn't even climb halfway up the *Billboard* Hot 100.

In January 1966, after the California leg of the tour (at Berkeley, four of Bobby Neuwirth's abstract paintings had provided a stage backdrop), the musicians went back into the studios in New York to record the first songs for what would become a double-album titled *Blonde on Blonde*. 'One of Us Must Know (Sooner or Later)' was out as a

© DON PAULSEN/MICHAEL OCHS ARCHIVES

SONNY AND CHER WERE AMONG MANY ARTISTS WHO JUMPED ON THE FOLK-ROCK BANDWAGON. LIKE THE BYRDS' 'MR TAMBOURINE MAN' AND BARRY MCGUIRE'S 'EVE OF DESTRUCTION', THEIR 'I GOT YOU, BABE' WAS A BIGGER HIT THAN ANY OF DYLAN'S OWN SINGLES.

single within weeks; the version of 'Visions of Johanna', a dark interior monologue set to a dirge-like tune, was put on the shelf. So was the incomplete version of 'She's Your Lover Now', which might have become part four of the 'Like a Rolling Stone' sequence. In February and March, working around the tour dates, Bob Johnston took Dylan, Robertson and Kooper down to Nashville, where he assembled a group of expert country musicians to accompany them. Notable among these were the guitarist Joe South, the multi-instrumentalist Charlie McCoy (who had already been up to New York at Johnston's behest to play on the released version of 'Desolation Row') and the drummer Kenny Buttrey. Somehow, the unlikely chemistry worked: the country musicians and the young folk-blues-rockers came up with a blend that borrowed the colours of all the idioms involved, but none of the clichés. The sound was softer and more contained than the music Dylan was making with the Hawks, but none the less potent. 'Pledging My Time' was a twelve-bar blues, but was it a country blues, a folk blues, a rock blues or what? It didn't matter: it was a *Blonde on Blonde* blues. In six days, thirteen songs were laid down, all good enough to find a place

AL KOOPER, DYLAN AND DOUG SAHM OF THE SIR DOUGLAS QUINTET ('SHE'S ABOUT A MOVER') IN 1966.

on the double-album. They ranged from the jokey ('Rainy Day Women #12 & 35', with its chorus of 'Everybody must get stoned!' and its Salvation Army trombone) through the lilting ('I Want You') to the driven ('Memphis Blues Again') and the reverent ('Sad-Eyed Lady of the Lowlands', subsequently revealed as a love song to his new wife). There were occasional wrong notes and misunderstandings, but the songs created and held a striking mood. As an extended display of Dylan's expressive range, it was enormously impressive. A dozen years later, he described these songs as 'the closest I ever got to the sound I hear in my mind . . . It's that thin, that wild mercury sound. It's metallic and bright gold, with whatever

that conjures up. That's my particular sound.'

Edie Sedgwick found out about Bob Dylan's secret marriage many weeks after it had taken place, and some time after she had signed herself up to Albert Grossman's management company at Dylan's behest. Dylan and Grossman had lured her away from the Warhol camp – which displeased many Factory people, who thought they meant her no good.

Warhol in particular felt badly betrayed by the girl he'd looked on as his greatest superstar, and who had appeared in several of his early movies – *My Hustler* and *Ciao! Manhattan*. Paul Morrissey, who directed most of them, described how Dylan started coming round to the

Factory in 1965 to see Nico, a German-born singer he'd met in Europe, and to whom he'd given an unrecorded song, 'I'll Keep It With Mine', which she'd released as a single in England earlier that year. Sedgwick did some dancing with the Velvet Underground, Warhol's protégés, who hated Dylan for what he had done to the Factory's sweetheart.

According to Morrissey, Dylan – who was now dividing his time between a new Woodstock house of his own and a room in the Chelsea Hotel on 23rd Street – started telling Edie to leave Warhol, urging her to sign with Grossman. 'She said, "I'm going to make a film, and I'm supposed to star in it with Bobby." Suddenly it was Bobby this and Bobby that, and we realized she had a crush on him. We thought he'd been leading her on . . .'

Morrissey described how Warhol broke the news of Dylan's marriage to Sedgwick, who was evidently traumatized. By 1971, she was dead. But if anyone was the Blonde on Blonde, if anyone was being held up to merciless scrutiny in 'Just Like a Woman', it was the girl whose story, composed of drugs and sex and beauty, made up the most perfect of all sixties tragedies.

D YLAN FORMED STRONG LINKS WITH THE
R OLLING S TONES, WHOSE DANDIFIED
RHYTHM AND BLUES MADE A POWERFUL
IMPRESSION ON HIM. H ERE HE IS WITH
B RIAN J ONES IN THE MID-SIXTIES.

DAVID BLUE (BORN DAVID COHEN) WAS AMONG THE EARLY DYLAN DISCIPLES IN GREENWICH VILLAGE, A MEMBER OF THE GANG THAT INCLUDED BOBBY NEUWIRTH AND PHIL OCHS.

IN DECEMBER 1965, DYLAN AND HIS MUSICIANS VISITED SAN FRANCISCO FOR A CONCERT AT THE BERKELEY COMMUNITY THEATRE. HE AND ROBBIE ROBERTSON (FAR LEFT) MET MANY POETS, INCLUDING MICHAEL MCLURE, WHO ASKED DYLAN HOW TO WRITE A HIT SONG, AND ALLEN GINSBERG (FAR RIGHT), WHOM DYLAN CALLED 'HOLY'.

On 13 April, a week after Dylan and Johnston had finished the mixes of *Blonde on Blonde*, the resumed tour arrived in Australia, where the newspaper reviewers reacted viciously to Dylan's stoned demeanour in the acoustic segments and to the dark, arrogant power of the electric music. Out in the Antipodes, they were behaving like the English had the year before. Was he, they asked, a protest singer? 'You name something, I'll protest about it,' he sneered. Over the next two months, he and the Hawks fulfilled a schedule of twenty-four concerts in Australia and Europe, made more punishing by the accumulation of interviews, drug-taking and mixed worship and loathing, as well as by the demands of the

music. 'Every night was like going for broke, like the end of the world,' Dylan said twenty years later.

Eyewitness reports suggest that he was now as tight with Robertson as he had been with Neuwirth the year before, getting stoned together, laughing together, staying up and playing and goofing and generally keeping the straight world at arm's length. Pennebaker was along, too, and filmed the whole thing, but the result, titled *Eat the Document,* was later suppressed by Dylan. So we have only the black-and-white still photographs to tell us of the hallucinatory beauty of this nervy, blade-thin figure with a corona of curls, bathed in a strange unearthly light at events in Stockholm on 30 April, in Paris on 24 May (where, on his twenty-fifth birthday, Dylan lingered with Françoise Hardy) and, finally, at the Royal Albert Hall on 26 and 27 May.

THE 1966 CONCERTS BEGAN WITH AN ACOUSTIC SET WHICH OFTEN INCLUDED ENTRANCED VERSIONS OF 'DESOLATION ROW', 'VISIONS OF JOHANNA' AND 'JUST LIKE A WOMAN'.

RIGHT: IRRITATED BY THE QUESTIONS AT PRESS CONFERENCES IN AUSTRALIA ('IS IT TRUE YOU DON'T WASH YOUR HAIR OR CLEAN YOUR TEETH?'), HE SNAPPED: 'THEY NEVER ASK ME THESE QUESTIONS IN AMERICA . . . THEY TRIED TO MAKE A CLOWN OF ME FOR THREE YEARS AND NOW I WON'T GIVE INTERVIEWS. I KNOW HOW REPORTERS HAVE TO EAT, BUT I WON'T LET THEM USE ME.'

DYLAN'S INTERVIEW TECHNIQUE HAD ACQUIRED A DEVASTATING SATIRICAL EDGE. 'I DON'T KNOW WHO I AM,' HE TOLD REPORTERS IN COPENHAGEN. 'THERE'S A MIRROR ON THE INSIDE OF MY DARK GLASSES.'

THE PERFECT BEAUTY OF THE 1966-MODEL BOB DYLAN CREATED AN IMAGE SO INDELIBLE THAT PEOPLE WERE STILL HOPING TO SEE IT WHEN THEY WENT TO HIS CONCERTS TWENTY-FIVE YEARS LATER.

© JAN PERSSON

96

© JAN PERSSON

© JAN PERSSON

ARRIVING IN EUROPE FROM AUSTRALIA AT
THE END OF APRIL, HE PLAYED IN
STOCKHOLM ON THE 29TH. ON 1 MAY HE
VISITED KRONBERG CASTLE, HELSINGER,
BEFORE THAT NIGHT'S CONCERT IN
COPENHAGEN. HERE HE IS WITH RICHARD
MANUEL AND ALBERT GROSSMAN (TOP),
WITH D. A. PENNEBAKER (LEFT), AND
WITH MANUEL AGAIN, IN A HOTEL ROOM
LISTENING TO A TEST PRESSING OF *BLONDE
ON BLONDE*, DUE FOR US RELEASE WITHIN
A FORTNIGHT.

© JAN PERSSON

ASKED IN 1991 WHAT HE WOULD GIVE BOB DYLAN FOR A FIFTIETH-BIRTHDAY PRESENT, BOB GELDOF THOUGHT BACK A QUARTER OF A CENTURY AND RESPONDED: 'THE POLKA-DOT SHIRT . . .'

The Albert Hall concerts – in front of audiences including the Beatles – are the most famous of all these legendary events, although time and overlapping bootleg releases have confused the accounts. Somebody yelled 'Judas!' at him one night. With stoned resentment, he replied 'I don't believe you . . . you're a LIAR!' and kicked the band into a treatment of 'Like a Rolling Stone' that became a hurricane propelled by rage and amphetamines. Somewhere there was slow handclapping, which he defused by mumbling inaudibly into the microphone until the culprits shut up. Where were these incidents – London? Manchester? No one knows for sure. One day, when the strange memories of this period are far enough from the centre of his heart, Dylan will change his mind about letting the world see *Eat the Document*, tell Columbia to disinter the tapes of the concerts and sort it all out. Then the greatest rock and

DYLAN SPENT HIS TWENTY-FIFTH
BIRTHDAY, 24 MAY 1966, IN PARIS, WHERE
HE STAYED AT THE GEORGE V, PLAYED THE
VENERABLE OLYMPIA MUSIC HALL AND WAS
FÊTED BY THE FRENCH ROCK ROYALTY —
JOHNNY HALLYDAY (*RIGHT*), AND
FRANÇOISE HARDY (*BELOW*).

REX FEATURES

PHOTOREPORTERS

ON STAGE AT THE OLYMPIA WITH ROBBIE
ROBERTSON AND MICKEY JONES, AND THE
AMERICAN FLAG.

© JAN PERSSON

FINISHING THE TOUR AT THE ALBERT HALL IN LONDON, HE TOLD THE AUDIENCE: 'I'M NOT GOING TO PLAY ANY MORE CONCERTS IN ENGLAND. SO I'D JUST LIKE TO SAY THIS NEXT SONG IS WHAT YOUR ENGLISH MUSICAL PAPERS WOULD CALL A "DRUG SONG". I NEVER HAVE AND NEVER WILL WRITE A "DRUG SONG". I DON'T KNOW HOW TO . . . THIS IS NOT ENGLISH MUSIC YOU'RE LISTENING TO. YOU REALLY HAVEN'T HEARD AMERICAN MUSIC BEFORE . . .'

OPPOSITE: 'I WANT NOW TO SAY WHAT YOU'RE HEARING IS JUST SONGS. YOU'RE NOT HEARING ANYTHING ELSE BUT WORDS AND SOUNDS. YOU CAN TAKE IT OR LEAVE IT. IF THERE'S SOMETHING YOU DISAGREE WITH, THAT'S GREAT. I'M SICK OF PEOPLE ASKING, "WHAT DOES IT MEAN?" IT MEANS NOTHING.'

roll tour of all time will be officially available for general enjoyment.

When the tour was over, Dylan and Sara went to Spain for a holiday. *Blonde on Blonde* came out in May, to general approval. 'I Want You' made a pretty single, and hovered on the rim of the American top twenty. In June he was back in Woodstock, editing *Eat the Document* and checking the final galley proofs of

Tarantula. Meanwhile Grossman, pleased by the initial showing of *Blonde on Blonde* in the US charts, went ahead with plans for an even grander tour, to start in the autumn. And on 29 July 1966, as Bob Dylan rode his Triumph motorcycle on a back road near Woodstock, he was blinded by the sun, panicked, mashed down on the brake, locked the wheels, flew over the handlebars, hit the tarmac and changed his life.

4. drifter's escape

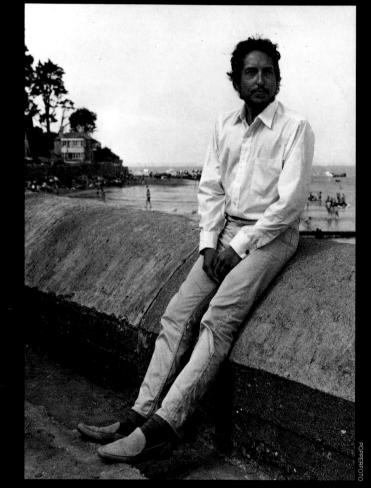

'As he lay in

a hospital bed,

his entire career

was dismantled'

Sara bent down to look at the broken, bareheaded figure. He'd been taking the Triumph to the nearby repair shop, and she'd been following in a car. It was obvious that he was badly hurt. At Middletown Hospital he was examined, and cracked vertebrae were discovered. There was mild concussion, and some bruising.

Everything went on hold. Gradually, as Dylan lay for a week in a hospital bed, and while he was convalescing at home, his entire career was dismantled. First, Grossman cancelled a big concert at Yale scheduled for the following week; the big sixty-date autumn tour was abandoned; *Tarantula* and *Eat the Document* were postponed. This is how Dylan later explained the decisions: one night in Woodstock, his injured neck supported by a brace, he had been sitting out in the garden, looking at the vista of rolling woodland, and had said to himself, 'Something's gotta change.'

When the news leaked out, the rumours began. No bulletins were issued, which

OPPOSITE: FACING THE WORLD'S CAMERAS AT THE ISLE OF WIGHT, AUGUST 1969.
BELOW: AT HOME IN WOODSTOCK.

106

made it worse. This was the time when pop fans were spinning the run-off grooves of the Beatles' albums backwards to decipher secret messages: everything had a deeper meaning, and the deeper meaning of Bob Dylan's accident was that he was dead. Or crippled. Or hideously disfigured. Or murdered. Or, perversely but most popularly, that it hadn't happened at all, but was a story invented to cover up his recovery from an overdose of whatever he'd been taking too much of on the world tour.

He did have visitors, some of whom told the story years afterwards. 'I know he wasn't as sick as he made out,' Donn Pennebaker said. Allen Ginsberg, to whom he'd been getting increasingly close during the previous year, brought him books and conversation.

Something's gotta change. Years later, he explained that he'd wanted to spend more time with his new son, Jesse, that he'd needed to slow down, that he'd had to dry out. As with his songs, there was no single meaning. All of these things were true, and a locked brake on a back road in the early morning had made them possible.

As far as the public was concerned, Dylan's withdrawal lasted eighteen months from

the day of the accident – plenty of time for the stories to grow wilder and more fearful. In fact he was back in action in April 1967.

Robbie Robertson and the other Hawks had stayed in touch, and by the end of the winter they'd moved up to Woodstock to join Dylan. Garth Hudson, Richard Manuel and Rick Danko rented a house in

West Saugerties, a plain two-storey breeze-block and clapboard A-frame painted an unusual colour, hence its local nickname, Big Pink. Robertson was in a house nearby.

As spring came, they began working together. Dylan, refreshed, was writing again. The musicians had set up their instruments in Big Pink's basement, where Hudson had

OF ALL THE POST-ACCIDENT SHOCKS IN STORE FOR FANS WHO LOOKED TO DYLAN FOR CONFIRMATION OF THE ATTITUDES OF THE SIXTIES, PERHAPS THE GREATEST WAS THE KEENNESS WITH WHICH HE TOOK UP THE ROLE OF FATHER TO THE FOUR CHILDREN HE SHARED WITH SARA LOWNDES. HERE ARE JESSE, ANNA AND SAMUEL.

WOODSTOCK WAS WHERE HE RECOVERED FROM THE ACCIDENT AND REASSESSED HIS LIFE. ITS RURAL CALM INFLUENCED THE SONGS ON *THE BASEMENT TAPES* AND *JOHN WESLEY HARDING*, AND IN TURN AFFECTED MUSICIANS AROUND THE WORLD.

© ELLIOTT LANDY/REDFERNS

wired up a simple half-track reel-to-reel tape machine with input from two or three microphones. And in the afternoons, they started making music.

Gradually, it emerged that this was anything but the pain-racked, amphetamine-crazed music of twelve months before. Away from the city life, away from endless travelling, away from the incessant curiosity of strangers, away from the need to keep up defences, the whole character of the thing shifted.

The four Canadians must have been crucial to this change. They had such fine control and far-ranging imaginations that anything seemed possible. They could switch instruments – Hudson to tenor saxophone, Manuel to drums, Danko to mandolin – with an ease and freedom that turned music-making into fun again, rather than some sort of desperate competitive sport. All of them (except Hudson) sang, each with his own distinctive sound, which made their harmonies movingly rough-edged, more like a black gospel quartet than the harmonies of a white pop outfit. Collectively, the sound acquired a rich patina of age, completely different from the neon-bathed glare of their pre-accident work. This was a major shift of emphasis: away from the modern, back towards

the sense of historical perspective that Dylan had abandoned when he began to go head-to-head with the fast-moving English groups.

Robertson had been encouraging Dylan to write in a plainer, more straightforward style. He played him Curtis Mayfield's lovely soul ballads and dared to tell the author of 'Desolation Row', 'How about a little less in the words department?' Between April and October 1967 Dylan seems to have written more than thirty songs, many of them in the makeshift studio, adding words as the rhythm section tongue-and-grooved the chords and rhythm patterns. Only two or three displayed hints of the intensity that had gone into the making of *Highway 61 Revisited* and *Blonde on Blonde*. Instead, Dylan's writing now veered from the playful to the nonsensical, turning what had once been a gallery of nightmarish grotesques into the characters from a neighbourhood bar, only slightly distorted. Things like 'Yea! Heavy and a Bottle of Bread' and 'Quinn the Eskimo' might even have been self-parody. There were some just-plain-pretty songs, too, like the charming, countrified 'You Ain't Goin' Nowhere'. The exceptions to the general good-time air were the aching 'Tears of Rage', a

collaboration with Richard Manuel; the menacingly apocalyptic 'This Wheel's on Fire', written with the assistance of Rick Danko and the Book of Revelation; and the lovely 'I Shall Be Released', the prayer of every innocent prisoner, whether his chains be real or metaphorical.

Sometime during the summer, Levon Helm rejoined the fold, and by autumn they were all making plans to record – not together, using the material they'd been working up every day, but separately. The Hawks had become the Band, a name reflecting their sudden pre-eminence among contemporary rockers. They'd arrived from nowhere to become the favoured accompanists of rock's most charismatic individual, and the legend of their prowess began to grow, pushed along by admiring fellow musicians. They signed a deal with Capitol Records and began recording their first album, *Music from Big Pink*, in New York with producer John Simon, later transferring to Capitol's Hollywood base.

As for Dylan, Grossman had renegotiated his deal with Columbia, persuading the company to double the singer's royalty rate after a protracted dispute which almost saw him move to a rival company, MGM. After signing the new contract,

Dylan hooked up with Bob Johnston and headed back to Nashville, scene of their triumph with *Blonde on Blonde*. Bassist Charlie McCoy, drummer Kenny Buttrey and steel guitarist Pete Drake joined them for three sessions in Columbia's studios in October and November, when the twelve songs for the next album were recorded. On the spur of the moment Dylan, looking for something a little less enigmatic than usual, decided to call it after the outlaw ballad he'd just written, which was based on a true character: *John Wesley Harding*.

Their individual labours completed, Dylan and the Band reassembled for their first public appearance since the Albert Hall. On 20 January 1968 they took the stage at Carnegie Hall to play their part in a tribute to Woody Guthrie, who had died the previous October. Dylan had apparently been the first to suggest holding the event, which raised funds for the fight against Huntington's chorea and for the establishment of a Guthrie library. He was joined at the two consecutive concerts by Jack Elliott, Odetta, Pete Seeger, Judy Collins, Tom

On 20 January 1968, Dylan turned up at Carnegie Hall for his first post-accident public appearance. As part of a tribute to Woody Guthrie, he and the Band performed three of the dust-bowl bard's best-known songs.

Dylan joined the final mass rendering of 'This Train Is Bound for Glory', Guthrie's anthem, alongside Pete Seeger, Judy Collins, Arlo Guthrie, Odetta, Tom Paxton, Richie Havens and others.

Paxton, Richie Havens and Guthrie's son Arlo. Wearing a dark-grey suit and the sort of scraggy beard and moustache that might have qualified him for a part as a junior apostle in Pasolini's *The Gospel According to St Matthew*, Dylan and the Band delivered three Guthrie songs – 'I Ain't Got No Home', 'Dear Mrs Roosevelt' and 'The Grand Coulee Dam' – making them sound like the songs they'd been recording the previous summer in the basement of Big Pink. The audience was packed with tradition-minded folkies, but now there were few complaints. For a finale, Dylan joined the rest of the singers in 'This Train Is Bound for Glory' and 'This Land Is Your Land'.

John Wesley Harding and *Music from Big Pink*, released in March and August 1968 respectively, turned rock and roll around yet again. While other musicians – Jimi Hendrix, the Who, Cream, Jefferson Airplane – were getting louder and wilder as the effects of acid and the trippy West-Coast philosophy worked their way into the system, Bob Dylan and the Band were very publicly opting for low volume, no distortion, an interest in the natural sound of instruments, a respect for history and a fondness for verbal formulations borrowed from

the seventeenth-century King James Bible.

The shock of hearing *John Wesley Harding* was as great, in its way, as the traumas of 'Subterranean Homesick Blues' and 'Like a Rolling Stone'. Instead of the great Gothic edifices of organs and electric guitars of the pre-accident months, here was a return to strumming, pure and simple: an acoustic guitar accompanied by a gentle bass guitar and quietly tapping drums, decorated every now and then by plaintive harmonica and sighing steel. Dylan was after the straightforward sound that he'd heard McCoy and Buttrey achieving with the Canadian singer Gordon Lightfoot (whose songs had been recorded by Peter, Paul and Mary). Dylan's singing, too, was markedly different. By his former standards of exotic phrasing and emphasis, his delivery of the dozen songs here was practically uninflected. His voice had become rounder, softer; although still recognizably Dylan's, it had been purged of all its many shades of anger, settling into a mood of calm resignation even when articulating complaints against the wicked and unjust, as in 'Dear Landlord' and 'I Pity the Poor Immigrant'. The title song was a simple cowboy ballad. The only lightning-flash of the apocalypse could

be glimpsed on the distant horizon of the tense 'All Along the Watchtower', and humour was reserved for the comedy of 'Frankie Lee and Judas Priest', a Keystone Cops recasting of 'Desolation Row'.

On the cover of *John Wesley Harding*, Dylan wore the same brown double-breasted suede coat that had been seen on the gatefold jacket of *Blonde on Blonde*. But whereas in 1966 he'd looked like a pretty beatnik, now he resembled a hick, incongruously surrounded by a mystified Woodstock workman and two of the Bauls of Bengal – mystical troubadours brought to the US by Grossman. Dylan looked uncomfortable, and in truth he sounded it on these songs of loneliness and flight, although their superficial gentleness fooled many observers into thinking that he must have found a haven for his restless soul.

Music from Big Pink wore its rock and roll heart more obviously on its sleeve, but it was still about natural sounds rather than feedback, about wood and valves instead of plastic and transistors. The Band's versions of Dylan's three best songs from the basement sessions were included: 'Tears of Rage', 'This Wheel's on Fire' and 'I Shall Be Released'; it also had his funny, *faux-naïf* painting of musicians on its cover, minus typography. But the spotlight went to 'The Weight', a Robbie Robertson song full of dust-blown imagery poised somewhere between the Old Testament and the Old West and seeming in the process to recreate some of the magical surrealism of *Highway 61* and *Blonde on Blonde*.

Between them, these albums rerouted the direction of many important musicians, from established giants like Eric Clapton to struggling tyros like Elton John. Even amid the high-voltage clamour of Jimi Hendrix's *Electric Ladyland*, the dark sexual charge of the Doors and the Velvet Underground, and the gleeful eclecticism of the Beatles' *Sgt Pepper* and *The Beatles* (the 'white album'), these comparatively still voices were required listening.

The effect was compounded when the recordings from the basement sessions were circulated, in the form of acetates, by Dylan's publishing company. Cover versions came in thick and fast, their makers secure in the assurance that the composer didn't intend to provide competition with his own versions.

Manfred Mann released a retitled 'Mighty Quinn', the Byrds cut 'You Ain't Goin' Nowhere', Peter, Paul and Mary claimed 'Too Much of Nothing' and, most memorably by far, the English mod queen Julie Driscoll performed a swirling Gothic-psychedelic reworking of 'This Wheel's on Fire' with the Brian Auger Trinity.

Dylan's absence had fuelled a hunger for his music which quickly found a new and highly unorthodox avenue of

BETWEEN APRIL AND OCTOBER 1967, DYLAN AND THE BAND WROTE AND RECORDED DOZENS OF SONGS, REASSEMBLING THE VARIOUS KINDS OF MUSIC THEY'D GROWN UP WITH IN NEW AND EXTRAORDINARY SHAPES.

IN COLUMBIA'S NASHVILLE STUDIO OVER
TWO DAYS IN FEBRUARY 1968, DYLAN AND
JOHNNY CASH RECORDED A SEQUENCE OF
DUETS, TWO OF WHICH WERE SHOWN IN A
CASH DOCUMENTARY ON NATIONAL
EDUCATIONAL TV THE FOLLOWING YEAR.

expression. Starting in 1969, the bootleg industry had found its first subject. The Basement Tapes, as Garth Hudson's informal recordings became known, made up the core of *Great White Wonder*, a double-album of unreleased Dylan material which also included tapes recorded in Minneapolis on the trips back from New York in 1961 and various early TV and radio performances. *GWW*, which is said to have sold close to half a million copies in various forms, was the precursor of hundreds of records and tapes documenting virtually every note Dylan had played in public, and quite a lot of what he'd done in private, too. His initial detestation of the practice was understandable — an artist should be able to edit his own output, after all — but it had no effect, and he was made to look hypocritical when, in 1991, with interest in his current output not exactly at a peak, he released his own triple-CD set of unreleased material under the title *The Bootleg Series*, thereby fulfilling many cynical prophecies made twenty years earlier by those who saw the original bootlegs as merely a harmless way of catering to an honest desire to hear more and more of him on the part of those who probably owned every note he'd ever officially released anyway.

Almost exactly at the time *Great White Wonder* appeared, Dylan returned to Tennessee with Bob Johnston for another series of sessions. In two days, with the *John Wesley Harding* trio plus two more guitarists and a pianist, he recorded nine of the ten songs that appeared on the next album, *Nashville Skyline*. The tenth, a duet with Johnny Cash on 'Girl from the North Country', was cut a couple of days later, during the taping of a TV documentary which featured the two of them singing Cash favourites like 'I Still Miss Someone' and 'Ring of Fire', backed by a group including Carl Perkins, one of Dylan's old high-school heroes. Cash and Dylan had been friends since meeting at the Newport Festival in 1964, when they'd sung together in Joan Baez's hotel room and Cash had given Dylan one of his antique guitars.

When *Nashville Skyline* was released in April, 'Girl from the North Country' led it off — and Dylan fans of every kind were appalled by the fumbling, stumbling job the pair made of that delicate love song, like a couple of grubby old drunks ineffectually trying to grope a pretty young barmaid. The next track wasn't much better: a brief and rather wet country instrumental. Then came a bit of strumming, Dylan's voice asking 'Is it rolling, Bob?', the beginning of a nondescript Nashville weepie called 'To Be Alone with You'.

The worst shock was Dylan's voice. All the edge had disappeared, and that seemed to go for his mind, too. What had appeared to be an interesting new reticence on *John Wesley Harding* simply dissolved here into mushiness. His idea seemed to be to find a voice that would pitch lines like 'One more night/The moon is shining bright' on their own terms, without adding any modifying or contrasting tone.

The album wasn't a complete disaster. 'I Threw It All Away' and 'Tonight I'll Be Staying Here with You' were authentically moving country ballads, carefully arranged with classical Nashville conservatism. 'Lay Lady Lay', written for the movie *Midnight Cowboy* but delivered too late ('Everybody's Talking', by Fred Neil, an old pal from the Village, got the nod instead), had the most interesting texture – a lush, swimmy mix of organ and steel guitar. Of the rest, who really needed 'Country Pie', 'Peggy Day' or 'One More Night'?

There was no reason why Bob Dylan shouldn't have been allowed to try his hand at singing like a truck driver at a Tuesday night talent contest in a very small town somewhere in Arkansas. After the rigours

and pressures of his life from 1962 to 1966, it was no wonder that he wanted to discover a more relaxing mode of expression. Perhaps, for a while, he genuinely didn't have anything to say. And from a distance of twenty years, it seems absurd that people should actually have lost their tempers with him just because he didn't feel like taking a fistful of drugs and singing 'Positively 4th Street'. But it was significant that he felt the sting sharply enough to defend himself to *Newsweek* with the astonishing statement that 'the smallest line in this new album means more to me than some of the songs on any of the previous albums I've made'. A decade later, he had a clearer view: 'On *Nashville Skyline* you had to read between the lines. I was trying to grasp something that would lead me on to where I thought I should be, but it didn't go nowhere.'

Such was the strength of the legend that *Nashville Skyline* reached number one in Britain and number three in the US, matching the performance of *John Wesley Harding*; 'Lay Lady Lay' was a top ten hit around the world. And it was the legend that drew almost a quarter of a million people to the Isle of Wight on 31 August.

Dylan and the Band had elected to miss all that summer's many giant pop

festivals, including the biggest of all – Woodstock – in their own backyard. But they were lured to the Isle of Wight by a persuasive pair of novice promoters who sent them a film of the island, complete with footage of the country house that would be put at their disposal. The money was good, too (Robert Shelton's claim of £20,000 plus fifty per cent of the gross take, plus £8,000 for the Band and £6,000 expenses, sounds plausible by the standards of the day). A few weeks before their departure, as a warm-up, Dylan sang four songs in the Band's set at the small

PERHAPS 200,000 PEOPLE WENT TO THE ISLE OF WIGHT TO WITNESS DYLAN'S RETURN. MOST OF THEM WERE DISAPPOINTED BY THE BRIEF SET HE DELIVERED. IT WAS AS IF HE FELT OPPRESSED BY THE WEIGHT OF THE CROWD'S COLLECTIVE MEMORY, AND BY HIS AMBIVALENT FEELINGS TOWARDS THE ENGLISH.

Mississippi River Festival, introduced as 'Elmer Johnson'.

His arrival in Britain caused a considerable commotion in the papers; they remembered the sparring sessions of 1965 and 1966. But at a twenty-minute press conference, Dylan was as limp as the songs on his latest LP. It was a telling foretaste of what was to come in one of rock's biggest anti-climaxes.

Dylan didn't help matters by taking the stage more than two hours late. Timing is crucial at open-air festivals, and if he'd appeared at 7.30pm, as scheduled, he'd have caught the twilight (a great advantage, as Elton John glumly discovered one summer night six years later, when he found his audience leaving Wembley Stadium after the Beach Boys had enjoyed the benefit of the late-afternoon slot). But Dylan's set didn't start until 10pm, by which time the huge audience was bored and irritated. The reason for his lateness has never been explained (in fact, he had insisted on being paid in advance, in cash, and when one of the crew was ordered to go and find out what was delaying him, he opened the dressing-room door to find Dylan and Grossman down on their knees, emptying pound notes out of plastic buckets and counting them into piles).

The Band kicked off with a short set, and at about 10.45pm Dylan appeared, dressed – to the general astonishment of those whose last vision of him had been of a skinny black-clad

POPPERFOTO

amphetamine angel – in a baggy white suit and a pale shirt buttoned at the neck. He did seventeen songs in his new soft crooning voice, of which the most interesting choices were the traditional 'Wild Mountain Thyme' and 'Minstrel Boy'. He started with 'She Belongs to Me', ended with 'Rainy Day Women # 12 & 35', peaked briefly with 'Like a Rolling Stone', but never encouraged Robertson, Helm and the rest to open the throttles more than half-way. When he left at about midnight, no one who had sat through the two-hour delay

could quite believe that he considered he'd done his stuff. The compère apologized. The newspapermen sharpened their barbs.

When Dylan reached the safety of Kennedy Airport, he told waiting New York reporters that he never wanted to go back to England again. 'They make too much of singers there,' he said.

If his subsequent thoughts are to be believed, it was in an attempt to make less of himself that, late in 1969, he moved house and started his next record. He had a son and daughter now, as well as Sara's daughter from her first marriage, whom he'd adopted. What he hated, it seemed, was the whole Woodstock Nation thing, and the pressure it put on him to be a symbol.

'We had to get out of there,' he said. 'This was just about the time of the Woodstock Festival, which was the sum total of all this bullshit. And it seemed to have something to do with me, this Woodstock Nation, and everything it represented. So we couldn't *breathe*. I got very resentful about the whole thing, and we got outta there.' He was also cutting his ties with Grossman, which made it convenient to move the family back to New York, to a house in Greenwich Village. 'Lookin' back, it really was a stupid thing to do. But

there was a house available on MacDougal Street, and I always remembered that as a nice place. But it wasn't the same when we got back. The Woodstock Nation had overtaken MacDougal Street also.'

It was in a further attempt to get away from his old fans, he claimed, that he went back to Nashville to prepare the double-album called *Self Portrait*: 'I said, I wish these people would just *forget* about me. I wanna do something they *can't* possibly like, they *can't* relate to.' They tried, though. When it came out in June 1970, they tried through the children's songs ('All the Tired Horses'), the *Skyline*-style country ballads ('Take Me As I Am'), the eccentric instrumentals ('Wigwam'), the bizarre versions of classics, both old ('Blue Moon') and new ('The Boxer'), the weird twenties picnic ditties ('The Star of Belle Isle'), and four virtually worthless items from the Isle of Wight. Yet, because he couldn't help himself, they were rewarded with a few gems: a beautifully tender 'Let It Be Me', a lilting 'Early Morning Rain', a heartfelt 'I Forgot More Than You'll Ever Know About Love', a reasonably alert 'Living the Blues'. Still, though, his self-portrait had turned out to be nothing more than a series of masks.

Dylan with two-year-old Anna in Woodstock, 1970.

5. shelter from the storm

'So he hadn't rolled up the past behind him, after all'

Uneasily relocated in Greenwich Village, Dylan had a better idea. Why not sound like most people's idea of Bob Dylan again? Back in the city, he'd been running into old friends and making a few new ones. Al Kooper, the hero of 'Like a Rolling Stone', was around. In two bunches of sessions, in the spring and autumn of 1970, he cut the tracks that were released in October as *New Morning*. Bob Johnston was to be credited as producer, but Kooper effectively ran the sessions.

At the time, it seemed like a miracle. Dylan may have been suffering from a heavy head cold on some of the songs, but he'd abandoned the plummy crooning that had afflicted his country recordings. His voice had lost a stone and a half, and to match it the songs carried less padding. There wasn't much that you'd call actual fire, but at least he was dealing in allegory and metaphor again. 'Day of the Locusts' spoke of the uneasy experience of picking up an honorary doctorate of music at Princeton University that summer, the citation describing his music as 'the authentic expression of the

disturbed and concerned conscience of young America'. By contrast, 'Went to See the Gypsy' took its inspiration from a visit to Elvis Presley in Las Vegas, blending the incident with his memories of the effect 'Heartbreak Hotel' and 'Hound Dog' had on the Minnesota schoolboy. The song 'New Morning' had more inner vitality than anything he'd done since *John Wesley Harding*, with Kooper's characteristic organ wailing away and a guitar solo by Ron Cornelius that was one of the finest individual instrumental contributions ever heard on a Dylan record.

There were oddities and disappointments, but they tended to be overlooked in the general desire to welcome him back to the land of living rock and roll. 'If Dogs Run Free' was a cod-jazz recitation, located somewhere between what Jack Kerouac had done and what Tom Waits was yet to do. 'Three Angels' was a talking hillbilly piece, with a heavenly choir which was also heard on 'Winterlude', a song as dippy as anything on *Self Portrait*. But, significantly, 'Father of Night', a ninety-second prayer, was his first unobscured expression of

faith, fast and direct, without a shred of irony or distance.

Part of the way through 'Went to See the Gypsy', a peculiar thing happened. The drummer, Billy Mundi, was misled by Dylan's clumping piano figures into turning the beat around – the sort of *faux pas* that would make any other artist halt the take. Not Dylan. Perfection had nothing to do with his attitude to getting his songs out, an attitude that has often lent a special vigour to his records. With *New Morning*, most critics expressed pleasure in the arrival of a record containing some of his old characteristics; it sounded better at the time, though, than it does today.

The worst aspect of his life in the Village in 1970 was the fact that he was being beseiged by a bunch of crazies led by A.J. Weberman, leader of something called the 'Dylan Liberation Front' and professed compiler of a 'concordance' of every word in every Dylan song, cross-referenced and analysed for its symbolic intent. To Weberman and his small group of friends, Dylan was a fallen prophet of the revolution who deserved to have his life made a misery.

They lay in wait outside his house, harangued him at every opportunity, and made forays into his dustbins in search of evidence that might incriminate their one-time idol as a born-again agent of neo-fascist *Amerika*. (The practice of 'garbology', pioneered by Weberman, surfaced again in the early 1990s in the guise of a journalistic stunt.) Eventually, according to Weberman, who affected surprise while telling the tale, Dylan lost his temper and decked his tormentor. It made him more determined to relinquish the idea of resettling in downtown Manhattan.

In February 1971, *Eat the Document*, originally commissioned by ABC-TV but abandoned by the network as the project bogged down, received its only screening, at a Village cinema – in a version edited by Dylan with the cameraman Howard Alk, rather than by Pennebaker, who had himself put together a more conventional narrative documentary than the oblique Dylan/Alk effort. They'd cut it, Dylan said, 'fast on the eye'.

Almost simultaneously, Macmillan finally published another leftover from the pre-accident era: *Tarantula*, a slim volume described on its flyleaf as 'Bob Dylan's first book, the only book he has ever written. He wrote it in 1966.' Dylan probably hadn't wanted to publish it, but his hand had been forced by the bootleggers, who had moved on from vinyl and acquired a manuscript of the 'novel'. Soon, copies with colour-xeroxed covers were available on stalls from Greenwich Village to Portobello Road (where it cost 25p – about 50 cents). 'For Dylan to permit the release of the book now,' Robert Christgau noted in the *New York Review of Books*, 'is to acknowledge the loss of a battle in his never-ending war for privacy.' Had it been published in 1966, it would probably have received something warmer than the tepid response waiting for it in 1971. The text began well – who could resist the first four words: 'aretha/crystal jukebox queen . . .'? – but sank into a stream-of-consciousness morass that would have been far easier to take with the *Blonde on Blonde* band in the background. Those who persisted found one particularly striking verse interlude:

here lies bob dylan
murdered
from behind
by trembling flesh
who after being refused by
   Lazarus,
jumped on him
for solitude
but was amazed to discover

that he was already
a streetcar &
that was exactly the end
of bob dylan

he now lies in Mrs Actually's
beauty parlour
God rest his soul
& his rudeness . . .

here lies bob dylan
demolished by Vienna
   politeness –
which will now claim to have
   invented him
the cool people can
now write Fugues about him
& Cupid can now kick over
   his kerosene lamp –
– bob dylan – killed by a
   discarded Oedipus
who turned
around
to investigate a ghost
& discovered that
the ghost too
was more than one person

Dylan was back in the studios in March, now without Bob Johnston. Leon Russell, who had graduated from the Hollywood studios to become the close associate of rock aristos like George Harrison and Eric Clapton, produced the session, as well as playing piano. Two tracks were recorded, with Russell's own rhythm section. One of them, 'Watching the River Flow', a rather nondescript boogie with a lyric interestingly equating contentment with a lack of

LEON RUSSELL PLAYED BASS BEHIND DYLAN IN THE BRIEF BUT MAGICAL SETS AT GEORGE HARRISON'S CONCERTS FOR BANGLADESH IN MADISON SQUARE GARDEN ON 1 AUGUST 1971. RUSSELL'S OWN VERSION OF 'HARD RAIN', ON HIS SECOND SOLO ALBUM, WAS AMONG THE MOST POWERFUL OF ALL DYLAN COVERS.

artistic inspiration ('What's the matter with me? I don't have much to say' ran the opening line), was released as a single in June. On its B-side appeared a solo version of the old song 'Spanish is the Loving Tongue', with Dylan singing and playing piano, cut during one of the *Self Portrait* sessions. Carefully paced and sung with affecting gentleness, this was one of his most likeable recorded performances.

In May, Dylan visited Israel for the first time. Fatherhood, and his own father's death in 1968, seem to have encouraged him towards a deeper contemplation of spiritual affairs. It was probably inevitable that, sooner or later, he would begin to think about his Jewishness – something that had never preoccupied him before. Visiting the Wailing Wall and other historic locations, he was impressed, and even investigated the possibility of taking his family to a kibbutz for an extended stay.

Back in New York, he got a call from George Harrison, with whom he'd been spending time over the previous year. At Ravi Shankar's behest, Harrison was organizing two benefit concerts for the refugees of Bangladesh, who were being pushed towards oblivion in the conflict between the two regions of Pakistan. Both concerts were to be held at Madison Square Garden on 1 August, and the line-up so far included Eric Clapton, Leon Russell, Ringo Starr and Billy Preston, as well as Harrison and Shankar. Would Dylan join them? He was interested, but would confirm nothing. When he arrived, he looked so restless that Harrison was unsure whether he'd make it from dressing room to stage or head for the exit instead. 'I'd like to bring on a friend of us all,' said Harrison, crossing his fingers. 'Mr Bob Dylan.' Twenty thousand people held their breath as the spotlight found a slight figure in a blue denim jacket, with a harmonica holder and a jumbo acoustic guitar. They roared their delight. But what would he sing? Something from *New Morning*? From *Nashville Skyline*? Or maybe, if they were lucky, from *John Wesley Harding*? He started to strum, joined by Harrison's second guitar and Russell's bass. 'Oh where have you been, my blue-eyed son . . .' It couldn't have been more perfect. 'A Hard Rain's A-Gonna Fall', the song of earth scorched by human folly – written during the Cuban missile crisis nine years earlier – now became a completely appropriate comment on the inhumane oppression of the Bangladeshis. There was further joy when he followed on with more old songs: 'It Takes a Lot to Laugh', 'Blowin' in the Wind', 'Mr Tambourine Man' and a magical 'Just Like a Woman'. So Bob Dylan hadn't rolled the past up behind him, after all.

This was his only live appearance in 1971, but as it happened the world wasn't going short of Bob Dylans. The contest to find the 'new Dylan' was raging between the record companies. In the sixties there had been the Village crowd: Tim Buckley, Tom Rush, David Blue, Phil Ochs, Tom Paxton. Now there was a new generation, a mixed bag including Steve Forbert, David Ackles, John Prine, Loudon Wainwright III, Steve Goodman, Jackson Browne. Some did well, others didn't. Most of them suffered from the shadow Bob Dylan threw.

In November he made another gesture that, like *New Morning* and the Bangladesh concerts, suggested he wanted to keep having a go at being an older version of Bob Dylan. He wrote his first 'protest song' since his pre-electric days: 'George Jackson'. It was a tribute to a murdered black activist, and he recorded it in two versions, one acoustic and one with a rhythm section (including Leon Russell and Kenny Buttrey) and two backing singers. 'He wouldn't take shit from no one/He wouldn't bow down or kneel,' Dylan sang, before concluding: 'Sometimes I think this whole world is one big prison yard/Some of us are prisoners, the rest of us are guards.' A Bob Dylan whom everyone could recognize was back in action, but – as with 'Watching the River Flow' – the single simply wasn't distinctive enough to make an impact on the radio. Like *New Morning* and the Bangladesh concerts, it was as though he were trying to get an old muscle back into shape after a long period of disuse and wasting, an impression reinforced by his presence on sessions with various old friends and new acquaintances in clubs and recording studios over the next few months. Happy Traum, Allen Ginsberg, John Prine, Steve Goodman, Doug Sahm, Roger McGuinn and Barry Goldberg all found themselves briefly sharing a stage with a legend who seemed to be trying hard to get a handle on himself.

'Who're you?' asked Sheriff Pat Garrett, swinging his cold gaze across the cantina until his eyes rested on a small, twitchy figure with a wispy beard.

'That's a good question,' the boy replied.

The part of Alias, a printer's apprentice in a small town in Mexico in the 1890s, was invented for Bob Dylan by Sam Peckinpah, the director of *Pat Garrett and Billy the Kid*. Unlike the main characters, Alias had no historical basis; but as a figure within whom Dylan could both hide and express himself, Alias fitted a great deal better than the *Nashville Skyline* hat or the Isle of Wight suit.

SUDDENLY DYLAN WAS EVERYWHERE, HANGING OUT AND SITTING IN SOMEWHERE IN GREENWICH VILLAGE ALMOST EVERY NIGHT. ON 13 NOVEMBER 1971, FOR INSTANCE, HE WAS AT AN ALLEN GINSBERG RECORDING SESSION WITH (FROM LEFT) THE POET GREGORY CORSO, THE COMPOSER–FRENCH HORNIST DAVID AMRAN AND (ON FLOOR) ED SANDERS, ONCE OF THE FUGS.

Dylan spent almost three months filming with Peckinpah, Kris Kristofferson (Billy) and James Coburn (Garrett) in the Mexican town of Durango. It wasn't a time of undiluted happiness – 'My wife got fed up almost immediately,' he remembered ruefully – but he took the acting seriously and became fond of Peckinpah, whom he was to describe as 'a wonderful guy . . . an outlaw. A real *hombre*. Somebody from the

old school.' Dylan spent March 1973 recording the incidental music, creating a series of songs and instrumental pieces that perfectly complemented the film's elegiac mood. Peckinpah, however, had lost control of the movie just before the final cut, and Dylan was appalled when he discovered how his music had been hacked about and redistributed. Only a song called 'Knockin' on Heaven's Door' was in the place for

FILMING PAT GARRETT AND BILLY THE KID WAS A SLOW AND PAINFUL EXPERIENCE, BUT DYLAN, AS ALIAS, AND KRIS KRISTOFFERSON, AS BILLY, MADE A GOOD COMBINATION, ALTHOUGH ON ITS ORIGINAL RELEASE THE FILM WAS MARRED BY A STUDIO-CONTROLLED FINAL EDIT WHICH DISTRIBUTED DYLAN'S MUSIC AROUND THE MOVIE VIRTUALLY AT RANDOM. IT WAS YEARS BEFORE SAM PECKINPAH WAS ALLOWED TO RESTORE HIS ORIGINAL SEQUENCING AND RHYTHMS.

which he'd intended it. 'I was too beat to take it personal,' he said, but the movie wasn't rescued until some years later, when deleted footage was reinstated and some semblance of Peckinpah's stately pacing restored. Released as a single, 'Knockin' on Heaven's Door' gave him a sizeable hit and became a standard item in the repertoires of many other singers – by now a pretty rare experience for the songwriter whose new work had once been fought over.

Dylan had recorded the soundtrack in Los Angeles, leasing a house in Malibu, close to a tract of land he'd bought a couple of years previously, and on which he was now building a copper-domed mansion – Xanadu – for Sara and their children. He'd got away from New York again, and felt he'd found a better atmosphere. The music business – or at least the younger, more creative end of it – had relocated *en masse* to southern California. The Band were nearby, with a studio of their own called Shangri-La. His Columbia contract was up, and he started talking to David Geffen, head of Asylum Records, a young record mogul who'd started in the mail room at the William Morris Agency before taking on his first management client, a young unknown named Laura Nyro. In only four or five years,

Geffen had become one of the most powerful men in the business, partly because he could talk to the new breed of articulate singer-songwriters – the likes of Joni Mitchell and Jackson Browne – in their own language. He could hang out with them at their houses in the canyons, but they also knew that his priority was selling records, shifting units, dollars and cents.

Dylan signed a short-term deal with Asylum in the autumn of 1973, his first label change since Hammond had put a Columbia paper in front of him twelve years earlier. He thought his old label had lost interest: 'I got a feeling they didn't care whether I stayed there or not.' But Columbia responded to his defection with a dirty trick: their A&R department immediately packaged together nine tracks recorded in Nashville and New York during the *Self Portrait* and *New Morning* sessions, and released a record with shoddy cover artwork under a bland title. *Dylan*, as the album was called, consisted of a mixture of cover versions and traditional tunes, in versions that were either warm-ups or rejects. Its appearance did his reputation no good at a time when it was already in a sensitive condition, but *Dylan* wasn't really as bad as its initial reception suggested. The trouble lay in the

arrangements, which featured female back-up choirs: he himself might have been singing 'Lily of the West' perfectly well, but to have a choir chiming in on every chorus, repeating the title line, sounded ludicrously artificial to ears attuned to a funkier kind of music in 1973. For those who could get beyond first impressions, there was a deal of charm in his readings of two songs associated with Presley, 'Can't Help Falling in Love' and 'A Fool Such As I', and in a full-blown kitsch picture-postcard version of 'Spanish Is the Loving Tongue' – arranged for band and chorus with no reticence about the addition of Mexican colour. More seriously, the most valuable inclusion was 'The Ballad of Ira Hayes', written by Peter LaFarge, a singer and writer who had been a minor character of the Village scene in the early sixties, and whom Dylan later remembered with fondness as the best composer of protest songs: 'Whenever I think of a guitar poet or protest singer, I always think of Peter.'

Stung by Columbia's unfriendly action, he went into Shangri-La with the Band, and in three days the six of them recorded the tracks for *Planet Waves*. Originally titled *Ceremonies of the Horsemen*, it was eventually subtitled

'Cast-Iron Songs and Torch Ballads'. The album had more substance than anything he'd done since 1966, and the material ranged from the tense drama of 'Going, Going, Gone', a communiqué from the demon-driven world of Robert Johnson, to the utterly unexpected 'Forever Young', a benediction for his children. The taut, bare-wires playing of Robertson, Hudson and the rest, utterly relaxed and spontaneous, had a lot to do with the album's success; so did the fact that Dylan seemed to have a lot to say to, and about, women. Some of what we think we know about his relationships could be glimpsed in songs like 'Dirge' and 'Something There Is About You', but only the solo 'Wedding Song' welcomed literal interpretation. A song to Sara, it was recorded in a single take at the end of a group of the sessions. An unadorned expression of his feeling for her, it was couched in the artless formulas we all use when we need to express such things: 'I love you more than ever, more than time and more than love/I love you more than money and more than the stars above' was how it started, and it ended in the same register: '. . . and I could never let you go, no matter what goes on/'Cause I love you more than ever now that the past is gone.' The intent air

© 1974 FRED W. McDARRAH

and firm tone of his delivery left no doubt that an important message was going out as the tailpiece of *Planet Waves*.

'It was over before we realized it had begun' was Robbie Robertson's recollection of the recording sessions. He couldn't have said the same about the subsequent

American tour, which began on 3 January in Chicago and took in thirty-nine concerts in six weeks, finishing at the Los Angeles Forum.

The sense of anticipation aroused by the tour was intense. Special events like the Isle of Wight festival and the Bangladesh benefit aside, this would be Dylan's return to

MILLIONS APPLIED FOR TICKETS TO THE 1974 AMERICAN TOUR BY DYLAN AND THE BAND. HERE HE IS WITH LEVON HELM AT THE SPECTRUM IN PHILADELPHIA ON 6 JANUARY, THE TOUR'S THIRD CONCERT.

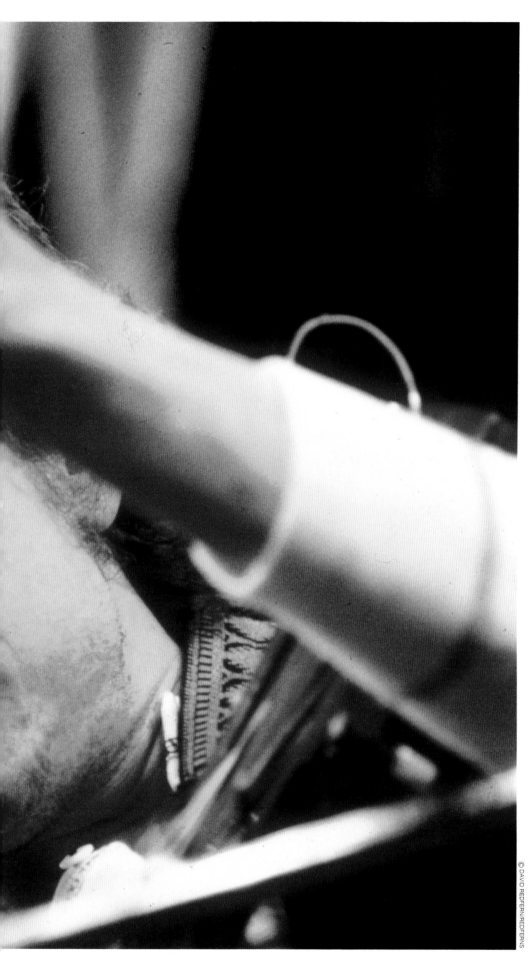

THE MUSIC WAS SOLID AND POWERFUL, BUT DYLAN KNEW THAT FOR ONCE HE WAS DOING NO MORE THAN REPEATING HIMSELF. NO ONE, THOUGH, COULD REMAIN UNMOVED BY THE AUDIENCE'S NIGHTLY REACTION TO THE NEW POST-WATERGATE RESONANCE OF THE LINE 'SOMETIMES EVEN THE PRESIDENT OF THE UNITED STATES MUST HAVE TO STAND NAKED'.

BEFORE THE FLOOD, A LIVE DOUBLE-ALBUM TAKEN FROM THE TOUR'S DATES IN INGLEWOOD, CALIFORNIA, AND AT MADISON SQUARE GARDEN, WAS THE SECOND AND FINAL PRODUCT OF DYLAN'S BRIEF LIAISON WITH DAVID GEFFEN'S ASYLUM RECORDS, A DEAL PROBABLY INTENDED TO SHAKE COLUMBIA INTO A RENEWED AWARENESS OF HIS VALUE.

activity as a public performer, eight years after his last tour. Bill Graham, the promoter, reckoned that he'd received applications for more than ten million tickets. Dylan kept his part of the bargain: the shows lasted two hours, included mini-sets by Dylan, in his acoustic mode, and by the Band, and spanned almost his entire history, from 'Blowin' in the Wind' and 'Don't Think Twice' to 'Something There Is About You'. The playing and singing were extrovert and powerful; this was an arena show, amped up and ready to roll, and it was greeted by the novel sight of audiences holding burning matches aloft in moving tribute to a returning legend. And as they crossed America, almost every night one line from one song drew a special shout of recognition: 'Sometimes even the President of the United States must have to stand naked' (part of the list of indictments that comprised 'It's Alright, Ma') fell with new force on ears that had listened to the lies and evasions of Richard Nixon in the years since the song was written. That moment was among those preserved on *Before the Flood*, the live double-album rushed out by Asylum four months after the last concert of the tour.

But there was something wrong. Good as *Planet Waves*

had been, the musicians weren't creating anything new on stage, just running with professional polish through a predetermined routine. They weren't surprising each other, and it was a relief to Dylan when it ended. Later on, recollecting the tour in tranquillity, he came up with a harsh judgement on his own contribution: 'I was just playing a role on that tour. I was playing Bob Dylan. It was all sort of mindless.' But since so many people had wanted him to play Bob Dylan for so much of his life, it was hard to condemn him for giving in every now and then. At least he knew a fake when he saw one.

Dissatisfied with life in Lotus Land, Dylan headed back to New York in the spring of 1974, trying to reorientate himself. He had been unimpressed by Geffen's apparent inability to sell more records than his old label, and the appearance of the *Dylan* repackage had made him nervous of what might be done to exploit his back catalogue, so he signed a new long-term contract with Columbia.

There was a dreadful, drunken fifteen-minute apearance with Dave Van Ronk, Pete Seeger, Melanie and others at a benefit for the Friends of Chile, organized by Phil Ochs. This was followed by

a far more auspicious event: a meeting with an ex-boxer called Norman Raeben who taught painting and philosophy, and who had been recommended by a friend in California. Dylan went to his classes for several months, and was profoundly affected: '. . . he didn't teach you how to paint so much,' he said. 'He didn't teach you how to draw. He didn't teach you any of these things. He taught you putting your head and your mind and your eye together – to make you get down visually something which is actual . . . He looked into you and told you what you were . . . Needless to say, it changed me. I went home after that and my wife never did understand me ever since that day. That's when our marriage started breaking up. She never knew what I was talking about, what I was thinking about, and I couldn't possibly explain it.'

He came close, though, with the songs that went into *Blood on the Tracks*, his next album. He was in pain, and he'd found a way of transmuting the feeling into art once again. There were few Dylan fans who didn't quickly conclude that this was his best album since the accident; straight away, it seemed to marry the poignant clarity of the *Freewheelin'* era with the complex emotional undertow of *Blonde on Blonde*'s ballads. Later on, he was angered by the general verdict that the album was strictly a meditation on his failing marriage. Referring to the song 'You're a Big Girl Now', he said: 'I read that this was supposed to be about my wife. I wish somebody would ask me first before they go ahead and print stuff like that. I mean, it couldn't be about anybody else but my wife, right? . . . you can't take my stuff and verbalize it . . . like, I don't write confessional songs. Emotion's got nothing to do with it. It only seems so, like it seems Laurence Olivier is Hamlet.' And then he said: 'Anyway, it's not even the experience that counts, it's the attitude to the experience.'

Giving him the benefit of the doubt, to which he was well entitled, it was possible to see in songs like 'Tangled Up in Blue', 'A Simple Twist of Fate' and 'Shelter from the Storm' an interpretation and analysis of experience: recreation is not the real thing, just like a report of a football match is not the match itself. He was

Watched by Dave Van Ronk (right), Dylan enjoys himself during a shambolic appearance at a Friends of Chile benefit organized by Phil Ochs at the Felt Forum in New York on 9 May 1974.

attempting something more difficult and worthwhile than simple reportage. He was trying to extract some wisdom, some lesson, from what had happened to him; to say that all he was doing was writing about his marital difficulties was to do him a serious injustice. He was going deeper than that.

Beneath its gentle, lulling surface, *Blood on the Tracks* seethed with thoughts and incidents to which Dylan's listeners could respond; their emotions were recombined and redefined, recalling the best from his past, such as 'Don't Think Twice' and 'She Belongs to Me'. Did he really loathe the object of 'Idiot Wind', for instance, or were these just the kind of things you say to someone you love when they make you crazy? And while 'You're Gonna Make Me Lonesome When You Go' is never mentioned among the lists of his great songs, he has never bettered that combination of a jaunty, optimistic tune – emphasized by his whooping harmonica – and verses about being abandoned. That kind of ambiguity, he was saying, is what life really consists of.

Blood on the Tracks was originally recorded in just three days at Columbia's A&R studios in New York, with Paul Griffin on organ, plus the members of Eric Weissberg's

band Deliverance: Buddy Cage on steel guitar and Tony Braun on bass. However, on a Christmas trip to Minneapolis Dylan listened to a promotional acetate and decided to re-record some of the tracks. Not standing on ceremony, he opted to do it there and then. With his brother David's help, he called up five local musicians; the rejigged album was in the shops three weeks later, with four tracks showing the evidence of second thoughts. Generally the new readings were brighter in both tempo and tone, although each of the takes that had been rejected in New York had its virtues. The new 'Tangled Up in Blue', and versions of it recorded later, showed how conscientiously Dylan was working away at these songs; the lyric changes were seemingly designed to make the whole thing more oblique, less explicitly based on personal experience, and he played with time-frames and identities ('. . . the way the characters change from the first person to the third person, and you're never quite sure if the first person or the third person is talking'). To balance the intensity of 'Idiot Wind', he included 'Lily, Rosemary and the Jack of Hearts', a nine-minute, semi-surrealistic narrative harking back to 'Frankie Lee and Judas Priest'. Taken as a whole, most

reviewers felt, this was an awful lot closer to a perfect album than anyone had expected from Bob Dylan in 1974.

Enthused by his first creative response to the new contract, Columbia's A&R department found little resistance when they floated the idea of another archive release. This time, instead of the sweepings from a bad job they suggested a proper release of the Basement Tapes. Under Robbie Robertson's supervision, a selection was made from Garth Hudson's hours of tapes and remixed in Los Angeles by the *Planet Waves* crew. Reid Miles, the distinguished former art director of Blue Note Records, set up a lavish sleeve photograph showing Dylan and the members of the Band in a variety of costumes, sharing a basement with a variety of characters – a ballerina, a dwarf, a strong man, a fat lady, an Eskimo – loosely related to the songs' contents. Everybody had some quibble about Robertson's eventual choice (no 'I Shall Be Released', no 'Quinn the Eskimo', whereas some inferior takes were included), and of course the bootleggers had stolen its thunder years before. Nevertheless, here was Bob Dylan not merely owning up to but also reclaiming some of his past.

6. rolling thunder

© KEN REGAN/CAMERA 5

'One by one,

figures from his

past assembled

at the rehearsal'

Perhaps Dylan felt that, despite his second thoughts, he'd given too much of himself away in the songs on *Blood on the Tracks*; perhaps he wanted to look outside himself for a while. In May 1975, on holiday in the South of France, he attended the annual festival at Les Saintes Maries de la Mer, in the Camargue, where gypsies from all over Europe gather to honour the Black Madonna. It gave him the seed of a song, 'One More Cup of Coffee'.

In New York, he moved around the clubs at a gathering pace, checking out musicians, sitting in, getting the feel. There was energy around: the young bands that were appearing didn't want to sound like Led Zeppelin or the Eagles. There was a new kind of radicalism in the air, a reaction against the way rock and roll had been commodified, turned into an industry. Dylan was from the older generation, but that was how he saw it, too. His answer was to put together a touring outfit that stood a chance of reproducing the spirit that music had possessed before every successful musician had been presented with three

roadies and a couple of tax shelters.

Dylan's Rolling Thunder Revue was a brave attempt to cut through the whole thing. It began when he stumbled upon a violinist, Scarlett Rivera, and found she had a sound that inspired him. In what must have been a magical day, she rehearsed with him, watched him sit in with Muddy Waters at the Bottom Line in the Village, and later went with him and the Waters band to visit the venerable Victoria Spivey, one of his first New York sponsors, at her home across the East River.

Dylan was writing more songs now, and his productivity accelerated when he met Jacques Levy, a New York psychologist and theatre director who had worked with Roger McGuinn in the late sixties on a project to turn Ibsen's *Peer Gynt* into a country-and-western musical called *Gene Tryp*. The musical never came off, but one of the songs left over was 'Chestnut Mare', for which Levy wrote the words, and which gave the Byrds a big hit in 1970. Levy and Dylan met in the street, hit it off, and began writing together immediately. The first night's work produced

'Isis'. Within a few days, they'd gone off to Dylan's house on Long Island, and very quickly produced nine more songs. These didn't have the intimacy that had been the most striking quality of *Blood on the Tracks*. Instead they tackled stories, going for extended narratives such as those depicting the plight of Rubin 'Hurricane' Carter, a black boxing champion who had been wrongly imprisoned for murder (Dylan had read Carter's book, *The Sixteenth Round*, and had visited him at Rahway Prison in New Jersey), and the life of a New York mobster, Joey Gallo.

For two weeks Dylan listened to musicians, and in July he went back into the studios with a new producer, Don DeVito – a Columbia staff man – and a motley crowd of musicians including Rivera, Eric Clapton, the singers Emmylou Harris and Yvonne Elliman, and the nine members of Kokomo, a British soul band signed to Columbia. The first sessions were a disaster. In the cellars of London pubs where they'd begun, Kokomo had been dynamite. But a big record deal and life in America had gone to their heads, and they weren't the band for Dylan.

In June 1975 Dylan went to Rahway prison, New Jersey, to visit Rubin 'Hurricane' Carter, a former boxer convicted of a triple murder nine years earlier. Dylan wrote the song 'Hurricane' and became part of the campaign that led to Carter's release in 1985.

Chaos ruled, until DeVito invited Rob Stoner, a bass guitarist who'd been backing Ramblin' Jack Elliott in the clubs, to help him sort it out. Stoner saw that the only solution was to throw everybody out and start again. Rivera and Harris were invited to stay, and Stoner called up his own drummer, Howie Wyeth. Now they had a workable set-up.

In a single session on 30 July they recorded eight songs, six of which finished up on the album *Desire*. By working with a small band, presenting them with new material and getting everything down in one or two takes, Dylan achieved — with Stoner's help — the spontaneity he has always loved. The sound of the band, though, was very much according to taste: for all its romantic keening, some

people found the constant presence of Rivera's violin too overbearing, too limited as a foil for Dylan's voice. Wyeth's drums were recorded with a much bigger, more emphatic sound than Dylan had used before; compared with Levon Helm or Kenny Buttrey, they lacked subtlety and individuality. Emmylou Harris was clearly at a loss in places. The task of watching Dylan's lips for clues as to the timing, while trying to read the words from a lyric-sheet, was not the sort of perfectionism she'd been used to.

The day after that session, Dylan called the musicians back and completed the album with the recording of one more song. Just as 'Wedding Song' had concluded *Planet Waves* with a hymn to his wife, now 'Sara' provided a coda to *Desire* – and once again the extraordinary quality of the song was its lack of ambiguity. It would be dangerous to take every line literally, but he seemed to be describing life with his 'radiant jewel, mystical wife' in plain detail, down to a rather dubious description of 'Stayin' up for days in the Chelsea Hotel/Writin' "Sad-Eyed Lady of the Lowlands" for you' which, even if untrue, was a surprising admission from a man who'd always scorned literal interpretation.

A few weeks after the album was finished, Dylan called Rivera, Stoner and Wyeth and, to their surprise, asked them to accompany him on a TV tribute to John Hammond in Chicago. Returning to New York, he took them into a rehearsal studio and used them as a nucleus while the remaining members of the cast of the Rolling Thunder Revue showed up. One by one, figures from Dylan's past assembled:

Jack Elliott, Joan Baez, Roger McGuinn, Allen Ginsberg, David Blue, Bobby Neuwirth and Ronnie Hawkins among them. New people included a singer, Ronee Blakely, who had starred in Robert Altman's movie *Nashville*, and four musicians who could play most things between them: T-Bone Burnett, David Mansfield, Steven Soles and Luther Rix. Their first job was to re-record 'Hurricane' with slightly different words, to satisfy

Columbia's libel lawyers. Cut at the end of a long rehearsal, the song required a dozen takes by exhausted musicians and was finally edited together from two performances by DeVito, which only partly explained the alarming acceleration of the tempo throughout.

On 30 October 1975, in the year of the American Bicentennial, Bob Dylan's Rolling Thunder Revue made its début at the War Memorial

THE ROLLING THUNDER TOUR WAS TWO DATES INTO ITS LENGTHY ITINERARY WHEN, ON 3 NOVEMBER 1975, DYLAN AND ALLEN GINSBERG STOPPED OFF IN LOWELL, MASSACHUSETTS, TO PAY TRIBUTE AT THE GRAVE OF JACK KEROUAC. GINSBERG SANG A LAMENT WHILE DYLAN PLAYED HARMONIUM, A PERFORMANCE PRESERVED IN *RENALDO AND CLARA*.

© KEN REGAN/CAMERA 5

Auditorium in Plymouth, Massachusetts – where the Pilgrim Fathers had made their landfall. A few nights earlier they'd finished off two weeks of rehearsals with a sort of pre-début at Folk City, celebrating Mike Porco's birthday.

Rolling Thunder played long shows, about four hours a night, with many guest spots.

The fifty-odd concerts they gave between October and the following May included countless variations – not least in the way the individual songs were performed from night to night. This upset some of the musicians, but pleased those who didn't want to settle into a rut and understood what Dylan was getting at. Part of the same philosophy led to

SURROUNDED BY FIGURES FROM HIS PAST, DYLAN ATTEMPTED TO TURN THE ROLLING THUNDER TOUR INTO A TRAVELLING THEATRE SHOW, WITH A CAST WHOSE FUNCTIONAL IDENTITIES CHANGED AT HIS WHIM.

© KEN REGAN/CAMERA 5

many of the shows being unannounced in advance. In addition, there were Dadaist tricks, such as dressing Baez up in Dylan's clothes and announcing her as him; Dylan himself wore strange whiteface make-up and a wide-brimmed hat, claiming to be after the method and style of the Italian *commedia dell'arte* troupes of the seventeenth and eighteenth centuries, whose characters (Harlequin, Pantaloon, Pierrot and Columbine) and costumes inspired Picasso and the French surrealist poets.

This whole spectacle was being captured on film. Dylan had called Howard Alk and told him that he wanted to pick up where their work on *Eat the Document* had finished. He thought he now knew how to make the film he'd failed with in 1966. A full-scale crew turned up a few dates into the tour, as did Sam Shepard, the young playwright whose work was already celebrated in New York and London, and whose relationship with Patti Smith had brought him into the Greenwich Village scene in the early seventies. The author of *The Tooth of Crime* and *Curse of the Starving Class* would have been a good choice to write and direct a movie featuring this cast: 'Rock and roll made movies theatre books painting and art go out the

AFTER THE GENTLENESS OF MOST OF HIS POST-ACCIDENT MUSIC, THE RAUCOUS STRAINS OF THE ROLLING THUNDER SONGS WERE WELCOMED BY SOME OLD FANS, WHO'D LONGED FOR A BIT OF BAD BEHAVIOUR.

window none of it stands a chance against the Who the Stones and old Yardbirds Creedence Traffic the Velvet Underground Janis and Jimi . . .' he wrote in *Hawk Moon*. But Dylan, it seems, couldn't explain to Shepard or anyone else what he wanted. Off-stage, he created little episodes in which the various 'actors' improvised dialogue that was sometimes based on their real existences and sometimes not – but he didn't

ALL WINTER LONG THE TOUR WOUND ON,
UP AND DOWN THE NORTH-EASTERN
STATES AND INTO CANADA BEFORE
HEADING ACROSS THE COUNTRY FOR DATES
IN CALFORNIA AND TEXAS.

have enough technique to get what he wanted on film. 'A lot of good scenes didn't happen because we had already finished improvising them by the time the cameras were ready to film,' he said later. 'You can't recapture stuff like that.'

The members of the Revue were not in general enamoured of the movie project. Sara, temporarily reconciled, had come along, and most observers thought that what Dylan was doing by using Baez and Sara as twin foils for himself was less than tasteful. What had started as a lark turned sour when both of them were pushed into the role of whores: 'The Rolling Thunder women all played whores,' Baez observed. Sara, too, was unhappy, and felt that coming on the tour had been a mistake.

Eventually, to subsidize the enterprise, the Revue left the smaller halls and entered the world of the arenas – although the shows at the Houston Astrodome and Madison Square Garden were held as benefits for the Rubin Carter defence fund shortly before Carter was granted a retrial (he was not finally to be freed until 1985). Everything seemed to go badly for Dylan in March, during rehearsals for the second half of the tour, when he heard that Phil Ochs, his old friend and rival, had committed suicide in New York; his marriage was on its last legs; and he was drinking hard. By the middle of May the show was falling apart, and its dying spasms were heard in the live album, *Hard Rain*, recorded at Fort Worth, Texas and Fort Collins, Colorado, with tempers audibly snapping. Musically, Rolling Thunder's finest legacy was the version of 'Isis' recorded in Montreal in December, when spirits were highest (seen in *Renaldo and Clara* and preserved in the *Biograph* boxed set). Wild and whirling, this was the maddest, the most delirious music Dylan had made since the amps were switched off on the 1966 tour at the Albert Hall.

The remainder of 1976 and the whole of 1977 were occupied by two projects: the finishing of *Renaldo and Clara*, and the fighting over the divorce. The movie was the easier: Dylan and Howard Alk worked away at assembling the material and cutting it down from what Dylan at one time envisaged as an eight-hour film to a mere four hours. Clearly influenced by his studies with Norman Raeben, the finished product played endless games with identity and chronology. Dylan was obviously Renaldo (although Ronnie Hawkins was Dylan), but who was Clara? Was it Baez, or Sara? Or both, some of the time? Robert Graves and Marcel Carné have been identified as influences on the film's themes and techniques; Dylan himself named only Cézanne. 'The interest is not in the literal plot but in the associated texture – colours, images, sounds,' he said. This wasn't what the major movie studios wanted to hear, and Dylan had to fund practically the entire film himself out of his touring income. It wasn't what the critics or the public wanted, either, and when it opened in New York and Los Angeles in January 1978 it was first savaged and then spurned. Pauline Kael's dismissive *New Yorker* review was ironically headlined 'The Calvary Gig', which was kinder than most. James Wolcott in the *Village Voice* called it the revenge of an artist on his groupies. It opened in Minneapolis, and then closed in all three cities for good, never again to be seen in America. The reaction in Europe was better, but not so much so that Dylan could live in the hope of recouping his personal investment in the most lavish home movie ever made.

Among the breaks in the editing was one for another piece of film work: an appearance in *The Last Waltz*, Martin Scorsese's artful documentary of the Band's farewell concert at Winterland in San Francisco on 25 November 1976. Appearing

RONALD GRANT ARCHIVE

THE SECOND LEG OF THE TOUR BEGAN IN FLORIDA IN THE SPRING BEFORE HEADING THROUGH ALABAMA, MISSISSIPPI, LOUSIANA, TEXAS, OKLAHOMA, COLORADO AND UTAH.

alongside Van Morrison, Muddy Waters, Dr John, Joni Mitchell, Neil Young and Neil Diamond, Dylan performed 'Baby Let Me Follow You Down' (a favourite from the 1966 tour), 'Hazel', 'I Don't Believe You' and 'Forever Young', before leading the company in a finale of 'I Shall Be Released'.

By comparison with *Renaldo and Clara*, the divorce really was a problem, and occupied a great deal of expensive lawyers' time throughout 1977, as Dylan and Sara exchanged allegations of bad behaviour ranging from serial adultery (his) to assault and battery (his and hers) in an attempt to win a financial settlement and custody of their four children – Jesse, Anna, Samuel and Jacob, plus Maria, Sara's daughter from her first marriage. Sara had finally left home after coming downstairs at the Malibu house one morning to find another woman at the breakfast table. Wherever the blame lay, Dylan provided a touching epitaph to their relationship: 'Marriage was a failure. Husband and wife was a failure, but father and mother was not a failure . . . I believe in marriage.' When the case was settled, in December 1977, the terms were not made public.

Both the divorce and the film were coming to a head when Dylan's new manager, Jerry Weintraub, booked him on a tour of the Far East, with an itinerary which soon expanded to encompass Australia, New Zealand, Europe and North America. Rob Stoner was called out to the West Coast in January 1978 and given six weeks to pull a band together. Dylan, who had been greatly affected by Elvis Presley's death five months earlier, seems to have envisaged a heavily arranged show along the lines of Presley's Las Vegas extravaganzas, with a big band and backing singers. Steven Soles and David Mansfield were retained from the Rolling Thunder band; Stoner called an old friend, guitarist Billy Cross, from Sweden; drummer Ian Wallace (once of King Crimson) replaced Wyeth; three session musicians, Alan Pasqua, Steve Douglas and Bobbye Hall, played keyboards, saxophones and percussion; and three backing singers – Helena Springs, Jo Ann Harris and Debbi Dye – were added. Together they worked out arrangements giving a new twist to some of his best-known songs, resulting in a reggae version of 'Don't Think Twice' and a heavy-metal treatment of 'Masters of War'.

When they got to Japan, CBS/Sony recorded the shows at the Budokan Theatre in Tokyo and put out a double-album which instantly became a collector's item in the West.

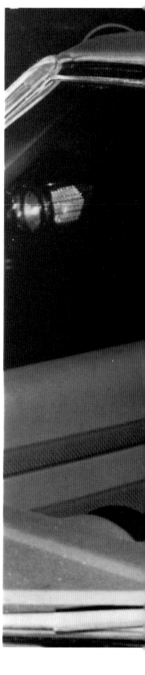

It captured something that, typically, had gone right to the other extreme from the Rolling Thunder approach. Now, instead of spontaneity, it was all about neatness and accuracy and giving each song a distinctive flavour. It was a show-band approach, and on *Bob Dylan at Budokan* he sounded as though he was doing cover versions – polite and distant.

Back in California in May after the Far East leg of the tour, the band – now with Jerry Scheff on bass and Carolyn Dennis replacing Debbi Dye – made a record that was something else altogether. *Street-Legal* may have used the *Budokan* format, but now

TEN YEARS AFTER THEIR SECRET WEDDING, DYLAN'S MARRIAGE TO THE WOMAN HE HAD CALLED 'A MADONNA' CAME MESSILY APART. LENGTHY DIVORCE PROCEEDINGS ENDED IN AN UNDISCLOSED SETTLEMENT.

Dylan was supplying the band with carefully worked material of its own. Some of the tracks tapped into his finest powers, notably the atmospheric 'Señor (Tales of Yankee Power)' and the relentless 'Changing of the Guard', a complex Tarot-inspired tale climaxing in a grown-up version of the rebellious injunctions of 'The Times They Are A-Changin': '"Gentlemen," he said, "I don't need your organization/I've shined your shoes, I've moved your mountains and I've marked your cards . . ." ' Now the band's sound was full-throated, topped by the urgent tenor saxophone of Steve Douglas, an LA session veteran who had played on the early-sixties hits of Duane Eddy and Phil Spector.

The musicians had performed seven consecutive dates at the Universal Amphitheater in LA by the time they arrived In England, for Dylan's first London concerts since someone had called him Judas. The atmosphere among the 7,000 people at Earl's Court on the

Rolling Thunder had given Dylan a taste for life on the road. In 1978 he took a big band around the world, beginning a routine that he was to find hard to shake.

OPPOSITE: IN NURNBERG ON 1 JULY, ERIC CLAPTON TURNED UP TO PLAY GUITAR ON THE ENCORES.

THE 1978 SHOWS WERE A JUDICIOUS REFLECTION OF HIS ENTIRE CAREER, THE EUROPEAN CONCERTS INVARIABLY CONCLUDING WITH A CROWD-PLEASING SOLO ACOUSTIC VERSION OF 'THE TIMES THEY ARE A-CHANGIN' '.

first of six nights was electrifying, all the anticipation fulfilled in a twenty-eight song selection that began with Tampa Red's old 'Love Her with a Feeling' and included only two songs ('Baby Stop Crying' and 'Señor') from the then-unheard *Street-Legal*. Dylan looked in pretty good shape, leading the band with confidence through the fast-paced set, the white lightning flash down the sides of his dark trousers perhaps a conscious echo of Presley's Las Vegas costumes. A few people took against what appeared to be the espousal of a new set of

© JAN PERSSON

147

Clapton was another veteran sixties rocker who found solace in the endless repetitions — plane/limo/dressing room/stage/limo/hotel/limo/plane — of life on the road.

149

WITH GRAHAM PARKER BACKSTAGE AT BLACKBUSHE, BEFORE THE CONCERT THAT CLOSED THE EUROPEAN TOUR. THIS WAS BY COMMON CONSENT ONE OF DYLAN'S FINEST PERFORMANCES. CLAPTON REAPPEARED TO PLAY ON 'FOREVER YOUNG'.

show-business values, but it was really nothing more than Dylan trying something different yet again – and anyway the whole thing was justified by the version of 'Like a Rolling Stone' played on the European dates, greatly evolved since the rather plain *Budokan* treatment; it now featured an ecstatic new emphasis in each line, underscored by the backing singers: 'You've gone to the finest school all right Miss Lonely/But you know you only used to get – *juiced in it.*'

The tour went on to Germany, France and Scandinavia, picking up favourable reactions everywhere, before returning to Blackbushe Aerodrome in Surrey for an open-air concert on 15 July in front of 200,000 people. This was everything the Isle of Wight had failed to be: thirty-three songs, including Sam Cooke's 'A Change Is Gonna Come' and Paul McCartney's 'The Long and Winding Road', plus six items from *Street-Legal*.

Back home, the response was not so favourable. Critics were more sensitive to the show's supposed Las Vegas stylings, and Dylan found himself yet again having to justify a new departure. He was feeling dispirited one night in November 1978, two months into the tour's American leg, when, in a hotel room in Tucson, Arizona, his life changed yet again.

WIDELY ACCLAIMED IN EUROPE, THE TOUR
FOUND A VERY DIFFERENT RECEPTION AT
HOME. AMERICAN CRITICS TOOK ONE LOOK
AT THE EXPANDED LINE-UP AND AT HIS
STAGE CLOTHES, AND ACCUSED DYLAN OF
ADOPTING A LAS VEGAS MENTALITY.

7. gospel plow

RETNA PICTURES

'People were
looking for an
excuse to write
me off'

In San Diego on 17 November 1978, someone in the audience had thrown a small silver crucifix on to the stage – the sort of thing that happens all the time to pop stars. Dylan usually let such items lie where they fell. This time, however, he had picked it up, and a couple of nights later in his Tucson hotel room, feeling down and disgusted with life in general, he put his hand in his pocket and found it there. And in that moment, or so he later said, the man who had once been among the world's most notorious sceptics became born again.

'There was a presence in the room that couldn't have been anyone but Jesus,' he said. 'Jesus put his hand on me. It was a physical thing. I felt it . . . I felt my whole body tremble. The glory of the Lord knocked me down and picked me up.'

It is possible that he'd been encouraged towards his revelation by contact with several born-again Christians in his touring band, notably T-Bone Burnett. A new girlfriend, Mary Alice Artes,

contacted the Vineyard Fellowship in Los Angeles, whose pastor sent two of his ministers to the Malibu house to talk to Dylan about his experience. Very soon he had enrolled in a three-month, four-days-a-week study class in the fellowship's School of Discipleship.

The Jewish boy's conversion to Christ clearly gave him some relief from the pressures that had borne down on him since he'd returned to the road. He studied faithfully, accepting the ministers' instruction that the end of the world was at hand. Before many weeks were out, the teachings had begun to show up in his songwriting. In May he started work on a new album, one that would reflect his current concerns. He recruited a brand-new team for the task. Jerry Wexler, the doyen of Atlantic Records' rhythm-and-blues roster in the fifties and sixties, was his choice of producer. Wexler, whose triumphs included the supervision of Ray Charles's finest recordings and the revival of Aretha Franklin's career, was the sort of producer who liked to put

first-class musicians together and let them get on with it. For these sessions, held at Wexler's favourite studio, Muscle Shoals Sound on the Tennessee River in Alabama, he invited his old friend Barry Beckett – the keyboard player with the great Muscle Shoals rhythm section – to act as co-producer, and imaginatively chose two men from Dire Straits, a new British group whose second album Wexler had just produced.

Although Dire Straits had come up on the same wave of energy as the British punk groups, their music held fast to the values of basic American R&B and country music. Mark Knopfler, their leader, was the most eloquent guitarist to arrive in years, a master of unshowy melodic improvisation. To him and his drummer, Pick Withers, Wexler added the experienced bass guitarist Tim Drummond, from Ry Cooder's band. The Muscle Shoals Horns and a vocal trio – Helena Springs, Carolyn Dennis and Regina Havis – completed the ensemble, the singers' work reminding anyone who cared to think about it that Dylan had listened to gospel choirs as well as folk and blues musicians in the years when he was absorbing musical styles like a sponge.

When *Slow Train Coming* was released in September, Dylan's audience could share the astonishment felt by Wexler, Knopfler and the others as they heard the songs for the first time in the run-throughs at Muscle Shoals. 'Gotta Serve Somebody', 'When He Returns', and 'When You Gonna Wake Up' were as strict in their admonitions as the oldest of old-time religionists. There was no escape; righteousness was the only route to salvation. The music was as funky as Wexler and his colleagues could make it: some of the tracks rode on a low-riding groove that suited Dylan as well as the spare commentaries from Knopfler's sweet Stratocaster. Nevertheless, cynics would sympathize with his new collaborators: imagine finding yourself at a Bob Dylan session, and ending up having to play on a nursery rhyme like 'Man Gave Names to All the Animals' instead of a real Bob Dylan song like, say, 'Stuck Inside of Mobile with the Memphis Blues Again'. The critical response was mixed: warm praise from the editor of *Rolling Stone*, a longtime supporter who had from time

to time revised his own reviewers' opinions; undiluted scorn from the new generation of punk-oriented journalists at the *New Musical Express*.

In November, Dylan took the new material on the road, starting with fourteen shows at the 2,000-seater Fox-Warfield Theater in San Francisco. No doubt boosted by the support of America's many born-again Christians, anxious to welcome the public conversion of a former Jewish atheist, *Slow Train Coming* was showing well in the charts, and to Dylan it was a matter of considerable pride that he could play a two-hour show featuring only religious songs (which meant that he had to write some more in a hurry). His band on this tour may have been, on paper, the best he had ever led: Spooner Oldham, author of several classic soul songs, and Willie Smith (keyboards), David Lindley and Fred Tackett (guitars), Tim Drummond (bass), Jim Keltner (drums) and the Jamaican percussionist Ras Baboo made a superb combination of flair and experience. Not surprisingly, though, at these and subsequent shows some members of the audience were disconcerted by the complete absence of pre-conversion material as the single-minded Dylan emphasized his intentions by delivering long, angry sermons between the

WHEN DYLAN TOOK HIS NEW GOSPEL-SLANTED MUSIC ON THE ROAD LATE IN 1979, IT WAS TO PERFORM SETS THAT MADE NO ACKNOWLEDGEMENT OF HIS PAST REPERTOIRE. A YEAR LATER HE RELAXED THE POLICY, ONCE AGAIN MIXING OLD AND NEW.

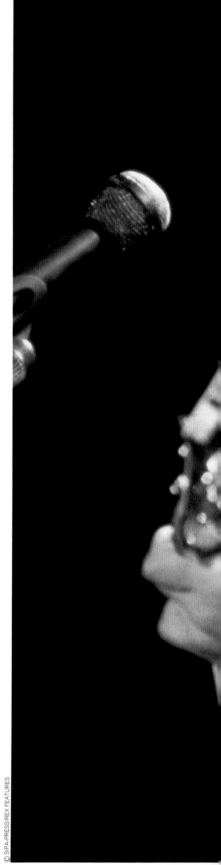

© SIPA-PRESS/REX FEATURES

songs. The reaction was mixed, but it was not as antagonistic as some of the more unfriendly newspaper reports suggested.

In February 1980 Dylan attended the Grammy Awards ceremony to pick up the Best Male Rock Vocal Award for 'Gotta Serve Somebody' – the first Grammy for the man who could point to 'Like a Rolling Stone', *Blonde on Blonde* and *Blood on the Tracks* on his CV. The ceremony interrupted sessions for a new album, *Saved,* for which he had returned to Muscle Shoals with the Wexler/Beckett team and the nucleus of the road band. Mellower than *Slow Train*, benefiting strongly from Spooner Oldham's sensitive organ-playing, the album seemed to be expressing a less intransigent philosophy, displaying in a complex song called 'In the Garden' the fruits of his study of the New Testament. The singers – in whose ranks Helena Springs, his lover from the days of *Street-Legal*, had been supplanted by his new favourite, Clydie King, formerly with Ray Charles's Raelets – were more cunningly integrated. And towards the end of a slow song called 'What Can I Do For You?' he suddenly unleashed a wonderfully intense harmonica solo, its swooping, side-slipping phrases recalling both the richly chromatic work of

Stevie Wonder and the architecturally complex style Dylan himself had toyed with in his 1965 concerts.

The cover of *Saved* featured a painting of the hand of God reaching down to the hands of men – a garish pastiche of Michelangelo executed by Tony Wright, an English artist who had created the cover of Bob Marley's *Natty Dread.* (When, in the late eighties, Dylan's friend Sam Shepard asked him which person he wished he'd met and hadn't, Dylan answered without hesitation: 'Bob Marley'.) Given a summer release, the album didn't match *Slow Train*'s platinum-selling performance, and Dylan later criticized the quality of the final mix.

After a five-month break, he returned to the Fox-Warfield Theater in November to begin a new tour, but this time old songs were included alongside the born-again broadsides. There were guest slots at the San Francisco shows, including the last public performance by Mike Bloomfield (hero of 'Like a Rolling Stone' and the 1965 Newport gig), who died of a drug overdose only a few weeks later, in February 1981.

In April, during another lull, Dylan began the sessions for his next album, *Shot of Love,* using his road band with guest appearances by Steve Douglas on tenor saxophone,

guitarist Danny Kortchmar, Benmont Tench (from Tom Petty's Heartbreakers) on keyboards, Ringo Starr on drums, Ron Wood on guitar and Duck Dunn on bass. Chuck Plotkin, an experienced recording engineer who had been working as one of Bruce Springsteen's co-producers, was brought in to help Dylan supervise the sessions. The two of them were joined for the title track only by Bumps Blackwell, the producer of Little Richard's classic recordings in the mid-1950s, songs that had affected Dylan more deeply than any others. ('Although he only produced one song,' Dylan remarked, 'I gotta say that of all the producers I ever used, he was the best, the most knowledgeable . . .') In truth, the religious phase seemed to be running out of creative steam, and the album contained only one really outstanding song, the slow, beautiful 'Every Grain of Sand', a his-eye-is-on-the-sparrow kind of hymn in which he and Clydie King let a gloriously gentle tune do the work ('I felt like I was just putting words down that were coming from somewhere else,' Dylan explained). As a whole, though, the album seemed to lack focus – a problem that was to return with a vengeance later in the decade.

PRESS CONFERENCES WERE STILL AN ORDEAL. INSTEAD OF BEING ASKED WHETHER HE REALLY BELIEVED IN THE WORDS OF HIS PROTEST SONGS, NOW HE WAS BEING ASKED WHETHER HE REALLY BELIEVED IN GOD. 'THERE WAS ALWAYS SOMETHING THAT PEOPLE DIDN'T LIKE,' HE TOLD ONE INTERVIEWER. 'I'VE BEEN USED TO THAT SINCE I WAS BORN.'

The 1981 European tour was widely seen as an anticlimax after the euphoria of 1978. On 12 July they reached Copenhagen, where (*left*) Regina Havis, one of the trio of backing singers, took her customary solo on 'Till I Get It Right'.

'People were looking for an excuse to write me off,' Dylan said of the response to *Shot of Love*, but really people were just getting tired of the preaching and tired of the sound of the gospel singers wailing away behind him with none of the flexible invention shown by real gospel groups – the Soul Stirrers, say, or the Dixie Hummingbirds. These singers were never really an organic part of Dylan's music, at least in the eyes of many of his fans, who would have preferred his voice to stand alone. Understandably enough, Dylan was offended by the negative response they received. When young audiences booed the singers' featured spot, as often happened, he compared them to the closed minds of the people who had jeered him in 1965 and 1966. But the singers were the symbol of what many saw as Dylan's loss of spontaneity and true feeling, which had been replaced by mere formats, both musical and spiritual.

A return to Europe in mid-1981 was less than triumphant. In Paris, while the CRS riot police played tag with the descendants of those who'd made a street revolution in 1968 to the strains of *Blonde*

LESS THAN FOUR YEARS AFTER DYLAN'S BORN-AGAIN EXPERIENCE IN A TUCSON HOTEL ROOM, HIS FANS WERE CAUGHT NAPPING WHEN PHOTOGRAPHS APPEARED SHOWING HIM WEARING A YARMULKE AT HIS SON JESSE'S BAR MITZVAH IN JERUSALEM. RUMOURS QUICKLY ASSOCIATED HIM WITH THE LUBAVICHERS, AN ORTHODOX SECT.

on Blonde, Dylan showed how many voices he could sing in while failing to stir much response inside the Stade de Colombes. At Earl's Court a few nights later, the audience grew restive in the gospel set and weren't much cheered when Dylan himself gave a drab performance which reached its nadir with a leaden reading of *Shot of Love*'s 'Lenny Bruce', a tribute of quite staggering banality. How could Dylan have included this song, with lines like 'Lenny Bruce is dead but he didn't commit any crime/He just had the insight to rip off the lid before its time', on an album that could find no room for songs like 'Caribbean Wind'? In the old days, when he'd

failed to include works such as 'Percy's Song' and 'I'll Keep It with Mine' on an album, it was because he had too much good stuff. No more.

When the *Shot of Love* tour ended in November, he shut the operation down for a while. It was time, it seemed, to take stock again; and for most of 1982 that seemed to mean taking a look at his spiritual life. Musically, no songs were released and no concerts were played, apart from a peace benefit in Pasadena with Joan Baez in March. Spending much of the time at his farm near Minneapolis, he ventured out mostly to see other, newer people – notably the Clash and Elvis Costello. Another lost year. This time, though the rumour mill ground slower and was only really in action towards the end of the year, when he was reported to be showing a new interest in Judaism.

In April 1983 he went into the Power Station in New York with a new producer, Mark Knopfler. The word was that Frank Zappa, David Bowie and Elvis Costello had turned down the job, but Knopfler, who had mastered every aspect of studio technique since Dire Straits' début five years earlier, should have been the perfect choice. With him came the guitarist Mick Taylor (the

Rolling Stones' original replacement for Brian Jones); Alan Clark, Dire Straits' keyboardist; and the great Jamaican rhythm section of bassist Robbie Shakespeare and drummer Sly Dunbar, the powerhouse behind countless reggae hits.

Released in May, *Infidels* made a powerful initial impression. The first song, 'Jokerman', signalled a return to verses laden with dreams and visions and symbols, carried on a propulsive arrangement with fine work from Knopfler's lead guitar and Dylan's harmonica. Another eight or nine songs like that, and Bob Dylan's career would have been on fire again. Unfortunately, the songs that might have achieved that had been left on the editing-room floor — partly because Knopfler left early for another commitment and was not invited back to participate in the final mixing and selection. What was heard were songs like 'Union Sundown', a piece of lazy thinking that condemned American capitalism for encouraging people to buy goods produced more cheaply in South-East Asia than they could be manufactured at home; and

OLD COLLEAGUES LEVON HELM (PLAYING MANDOLIN, LEFT) AND RICK DANKO (UNSEEN) INVITED DYLAN TO JOIN THEM ON STAGE AT THE LONE STAR CAFÉ, NEW YORK, ON 16 FEBRUARY 1983.

'Neighbourhood Bully', a simple-minded defence of Israeli nationalism. What we could have been given was soon made clear on bootlegs: the unreleased material included the pretty 'Something's Got a Hold of My Heart', an early version of 'Tight Connection to My Heart', which was eventually recorded for *Empire Burlesque* in 1985; the Tex-Mex 'Tell Me'; the moving 'Lord Protect My Child'; and the six-minute 'Foot of Pride', a slinky blues-with-a-twist with a dense, complex and clearly moralistic lyric that made it something of a latter-day equivalent of 'It's Alright, Ma'.

But the track that really became the legend of the *Infidels* sessions was one named after an old-time blues singer. 'Blind Willie McTell' was the title, and Dylan used the device of his narrator's admiration for McTell's music as the basis for a very personal state-of-the-nation address. Borrowing the format last used in *Planet Waves*' 'Dirge', Dylan played piano, with Knopfler on acoustic guitar, in a relaxed duet setting for one of his most impassioned vocal performances. The lyric seemed to summon up the country's whole history, evoking a world of mules and slave ships and hoot-owls and plantations as the prelude to a crunching conclusion, in which

the singer's own contemporary voice took over, yanking himself and the listener into the present: 'Well God's in his heaven/And we all want what's his/But power and greed and corruptible seed/Seem to be all that there is.' And then the final judgement on what's real and what is not: 'I'm gazin' out the window/Of the St James Hotel/And I know no one can sing the blues/Like Blind Willie McTell.' In this song, as in no other, Dylan brought off the trick of playing with time, which he'd admired in European art movies and had been encouraged to try through his studies with Norman Raeben. If he ever needed to explain why the anti-chronology technique was worth the trouble he took to acquire it, the great 'Blind Willie McTell', a song of incomparable vision carrying a far more powerful moral force than anything released on his 'religious' albums, would be all the evidence he required. Why he left it in the can until the release of *The Bootleg Series Vols 1–3* in 1991 will forever remain a mystery. 'It had a kind of broad landscape setting,' he said when taxed about his original omission. 'That was how it was envisioned, anyway. It never really reached that proportion for me lyrically. It never got developed.' For the first time, nobody agreed with him.

BROUGHT INTO THE *SLOW TRAIN COMING* SESSIONS BY PRODUCER JERRY WEXLER IN 1979, FOUR YEARS LATER GUITARIST MARK KNOPFLER CO-PRODUCED THE *INFIDELS* ALBUM, WHOSE SESSIONS CONTAINED DYLAN'S MOST IMPORTANT WORK OF THE 1980S. KNOPFLER WAS UPSET WHEN DYLAN MIXED THE ALBUM WITHOUT HIM, LEAVING OUT SOME OF THE FINEST SONGS. BUT IN 1986 THEY APPEARED ON STAGE TOGETHER IN AUSTRALIA, WHILE ON SEPARATE TOURS.

© FIN COSTELLO/REDFERNS

8. loose connections

'I can't figure
out sometimes if
people think I'm
alive or dead'

Bob Dylan entered the video age at the beginning of 1984, when he made clips to promote two singles: 'Sweetheart Like You' and 'Jokerman'. In fact, the first few minutes of *Don't Look Back* twenty years earlier might have constituted the original rock video, as Dylan held up and tossed away cue cards in an alley while 'Subterranean Homesick Blues' was played and Allen Ginsberg pottered about in the background.

In May he was off on tour with another new band, this one thrown together for a European itinerary consisting of big stadiums on a bill shared with the guitarist Carlos Santana and, at half a dozen concerts, Joan Baez. Dylan called up Mick Taylor, who brought along another British musician, the drummer Colin Allen. A third, Ian MacLagen, once of the Faces,

DYLAN'S EVIDENT ENJOYMENT OF TOURING WAS UNDERCUT DURING THE MID-1980s BY THE DIFFICULTIES HE EXPERIENCED IN ASSEMBLING A SATISFACTORY BAND.

IN MAY 1984 DYLAN JOINED SARA AT THE GRADUATION OF HIS STEP-DAUGHTER MARIA FROM MACALESTER COLLEGE. DAVID ZIMMERMAN, DYLAN'S BROTHER, IS ON THE LEFT.

After describing their relationship with touching dignity in her song 'Diamonds and Rust', Joan Baez joined Dylan and Carlos Santana for five concerts on their tour of Europe in 1984.

The concert at St James's Park, Newcastle, on 5 July provided two tracks for *Real Live*, a souvenir album notable only for a reworked version of 'Tangled Up in Blue', recorded at Wembley Stadium two days later, when Eric Clapton and Chrissie Hynde turned up to lend a hand.

played keyboards; the only other American besides Dylan was Greg Sutton, the bass guitarist. The rehearsals followed Dylan's usual formula, which meant a cursory run through dozens of songs that would never actually be played in concert, so that when the musicians took the stage in Verona for the first show they were still strangers to Dylan and the repertoire, and would acquire familiarity only as the tour went on. By the time they got to Rome three weeks later, they were, in fact, reasonably well co-ordinated. Dylan, dressed in black with big hair, looked more like himself, and sounded in control. A new, radically rewritten version of 'Tangled Up in Blue' was electrifying, even in the vastness of the Palaeur, a sports hall in the middle of a modern suburb. The six-week tour finished with dates in Newcastle and at Wembley Stadium in the UK, and at Slane Castle in Ireland, where they were joined briefly by Van Morrison, another seeker after enlightenment. At the end of the year, to no great fanfare, a souvenir album called *Real Live* was released, valuable only for including the revised, less overtly personal 'Tangled Up in Blue', with which its composer expressed satisfaction at last.

In December Dylan began

Van Morrison was one of the guests on the final concert at Slane Castle in Ireland on 8 July. The Belfast Cowboy joined in on 'It's All Over Now, Baby Blue' and his own 'Tupelo Honey'.

© JOHN HUME

work on an album that was to be called *Empire Burlesque*, but the sessions were interrupted at the beginning of 1985 for a one-off project: 'We Are the World', the American response to Bob Geldof's Band Aid scheme for drawing attention to the Ethiopian famine. Dylan joined in, alongside people like Lionel Richie, Ray Charles and Bruce Springsteen. When *Empire Burlesque* came out, it proved to be the weakest

album Dylan had ever made. It comprised a selection of mediocre songs recorded with a variety of musicians in several locations, but above all it was irredeemably compromised by the decision to give it all over for remixing to a fashionable disco technician, Arthur Baker, whose vacuous treatments were utterly at odds with what Dylan was about, both musically and philosophically.

On 13 July, London and

Philadelphia were linked in a worldwide satellite TV network to realize Geldof's vision of a charity event that no one could ignore. Dylan was chosen to close the US leg of the Live Aid show, taking the stage in Philadelphia in front of a worldwide audience of hundreds of millions with Ronnie Wood and Keith Richards in tow – three raggle-taggle gypsies beamed down from a parallel universe, playing very approximate

AFTER A DAY OF INTERGALACTIC GOOD VIBES AND WELL-DISCIPLINED CORPORATE ROCK ON 13 JULY 1985, LIVE AID WAS FINISHED OFF BY DYLAN, RONNIE WOOD AND KEITH RICHARDS WITH A SET AT PHILADELPHIA'S JOHN F. KENNEDY STADIUM THAT REMINDED A WORLDWIDE AUDIENCE OF THE MUSIC'S ROOTS IN RESISTANCE TO GROWN-UP VALUES.

© SIPA-PRESS/REX FEATURES

DYLAN'S CALCULATED AND CONTROVERSIAL REMARK AT LIVE AID ABOUT THE PLIGHT OF AMERICAN FARMERS LED TO THE CREATION OF THE FARM AID CONCERTS. AT THE FIRST, IN CHAMPAIGN, ILLINOIS, ON 21–22 SEPTEMBER, HE APPEARED FOR THE FIRST TIME WITH TOM PETTY'S HEARTBREAKERS.

versions of 'When the Ship Comes In', 'The Ballad of Hollis Brown' and 'Blowin' in the Wind'. Their conduct was either disgracefully irresponsible or magnificently perverse, according to where you stood, and they were heavily criticized for putting on such a sloppy show, although they could reasonably have pointed out that the monitor system had packed up and that Dylan wasn't hearing either himself or the others properly. Dylan made himself even more unpopular when he used 'Hollis Brown' to divert the audience's attention from the plight of the Ethiopian famine victims to the state of the Midwest American farmer,

another sufferer from agro-economic blight. He suggested that some of the money might go to them – 'just one or two millions' – and although he was derided for spoiling the party, his spontaneous initiative started the momentum of a Farm Aid movement, which, sponsored by Willie Nelson and John Cougar Mellencamp, eventually achieved just what he'd suggested.

In July, Dylan visited Moscow to perform for members of the Soviet Writers' Union at the behest of the poet Yevgeny Yevtushenko. In September, at the first Farm Aid concert, he played with Tom Petty and the Heartbreakers, after a long

A LONG WAY FROM DINKYTOWN: ON STAGE AT MINNEAPOLIS'S METRODOME DURING THE US LEG OF THE TRUE CONFESSIONS TOUR, 26 JUNE 1986.

© 1991 JIM STEINFELDT

Drumming up publicity for the *Biograph* box, on 13 November 1985 the Columbia Records president threw a party at the Whitney Museum in New York to celebrate Dylan's twenty-five-year career and thirty-five million sales. Guests included Lou Reed, Ian Hunter, Judy Collins and Billy Joel.

rehearsal session which Petty later described as 'one of the best times I've ever had'. Continuing his round of contributions to political causes, he joined in with Miami Steve Van Zandt's 'Sun City' recording, an anti-apartheid project. And on 13 November, at an evening in New York's Whitney Museum hosted by the president of Columbia Records, Walter Yetnikoff, and attended by Robbie Robertson, Lou Reed, David Bowie, Pete Townshend and many other rock veterans, he was showered with gifts to mark his twenty-five-year career and to give some promotional impetus to *Biograph*, the fifty-three-track boxed set chronicling the whole story. The box included a booklet based on interviews in which Dylan was more candid and illuminating than

ever before about his life and art, proving himself to have forgotten very little, and to have been his own best critic all along.

For the previous year or so, Dylan had been engaged in a legal battle with Albert Grossman, his former manager. Grossman had sued him for a million dollars, to which Dylan had responded with a counter-suit for seven million. Various court hearings had done nothing except enrich the lawyers. The litigation was interrupted when, on a London-bound flight on 25 January 1986, Grossman suffered a heart attack and died.

Dylan and Tom Petty had forged a friendship at the first Farm Aid concert, and in February they set off together on a tour that lasted through August and resumed the following year. Petty's Heartbreakers were a strong band, but in creative terms the two halves of the unit had little to offer each other, which is why the collaboration produced no substantial recorded legacy.

Knocked Out Loaded, another disappointing album, came out in July. 'It's all sorts of stuff,' Dylan said, with more accuracy than tact. 'It doesn't really have a theme or purpose.' In between a handful of Bob Dylan songs that Bob

THERE WERE MIXED FEELINGS ABOUT THE
TRUE CONFESSIONS AND TEMPLES IN
FLAMES TOURS. IN THE RECORDING
STUDIO, DYLAN AND PETTY FAILED TO
STRIKE SPARKS.

Dylan would never return to, there were collaborations with Carol Bayer Sager, Tom Petty and Sam Shepard. The track featuring Shepard, 'Brownsville Girl', was the album's only highlight: an absorbing, dream-like eleven-minute tale about a man remembering going to a Gregory Peck movie, and what it made him feel about a woman and a journey they'd taken together – something like that, anyway. The big, echoing production, featuring a Spector-sized snare drum, a loud brass section and the return of the wailing gospel women, almost drowned a funny, ruminative Dylan vocal that, like the song, deserved a better setting. The album's sloppy cover design alone was enough to suggest that at this stage nobody really cared about Bob Dylan's recording career, and that Dylan himself hadn't got a clue what to do about it.

That Dylan was still thinking about his own movie career became apparent in August, when he turned up at the National Film Theatre in London for an uneasy press conference to announce the making of a feature film called *Hearts of Fire*, in which he was to star as a washed-up sixties rock star alongside the young British actor Rupert Everett as a younger rocker, and an unknown actress, Fiona

REX FEATURES

RICHARD MARQUAND'S *HEARTS OF FIRE* REPRESENTED DYLAN'S ARTISTIC NADIR. FROM ITS EMBARRASSING PRESS CONFERENCE (WITH CO-STARS RUPERT EVERETT AND FIONA FLANAGAN) TO ITS ONE-WEEK-ONLY CINEMA RELEASE, IT WAS SIMPLY A BAD IDEA.

DYLAN'S LATE-EIGHTIES UNCERTAINTIES WERE MIRRORED IN A SERIES OF PUZZLINGLY ILL-CONCEIVED ALBUMS. WHO COULD DEFINE THE ARTISTIC DIRECTION OF THE EQUALLY CHARACTERLESS *EMPIRE BURLESQUE*, *KNOCKED OUT LOADED* OR *DOWN IN THE GROOVE*?

REX FEATURES

Flanagan, who played the focus of both men's affections. When it was released a year later, after shooting in Britain and Canada (and following the untimely death of its director, Richard Marquand), it lasted just one week in a single London cinema and was thereafter relegated to the video racks. Dylan couldn't even manage to compose a full complement of songs for the soundtrack album, relying on cover versions to pad it out.

Jamming with Michael Jackson at Elizabeth Taylor's birthday party in Burt Bacharach's Hollywood mansion was how 1987 started, followed by a performance of Gershwin's 'Soon' at a concert at the Brooklyn Academy of Music to mark the fiftieth anniversary of the composer's death. In April Dylan was on stage with U2 in Los Angeles and in July he appeared in a short tour of major American stadiums as the lead singer with the Grateful Dead.

An idea that had arisen from a couple of enjoyable jams during the tour with the Heartbreakers the previous year, the partnership with the Dead didn't work out. Dylan's anarchic rehearsal technique threw the finely grooved old hippies into confusion. 'It was not our finest hour, nor his,' said the Dead's drummer, Mickey Hart. But the guitarist

Jerry Garcia summed up the man fondly: 'Dylan has written songs that touch into places people have never sung about before. And to me that's tremendously powerful. And also, because he's an old folkie, he sometimes writes a beautiful melody. He doesn't always *sing* it, but it's there.'

But *Dylan and the Dead*, the live album which appeared more than a year later, was an unwanted souvenir of a best-forgotten collaboration – except that, utterly unnoticed, it contained a version of *Highway 61 Revisited*'s 'Queen Jane Approximately' which, in its wrecked majesty, came as close as Kooper, Bloomfield, Robertson and Hudson ever did to 'that thin, that wild mercury sound, metallic and bright gold, with whatever that conjures up'. It was an authentic Dylan classic, endlessly listenable, marooned in a sea of dross.

On 20 January 1988, Bruce Springsteen – the only man to survive and prosper after being labelled the 'new Dylan' – stepped up to the microphone on a New York stage and told a music business audience: 'The first time I heard Bob Dylan, I was in the car with my mother listening to WMCA and on came that snare shot that sounded like somebody'd kicked open the

HARDLY ANYBODY ENJOYED DYLAN'S SIX-
CONCERT TOUR WITH THE GRATEFUL DEAD
IN JULY 1987, ALTHOUGH THE ADVENTURE
WAS TO BE JUSTIFIED BY THE INCLUSION IN
THE DELAYED SOUVENIR ALBUM OF ONE
PERFORMANCE OF CLASSIC PROPORTIONS.

door to your mind . . . "Like a Rolling Stone". My mother – she was no stiff with rock and roll, she liked the music – sat there for a minute, then looked at me and said: "That guy can't sing." But I knew she was wrong. I sat there and I didn't say nothing but I knew that I was listening to the toughest voice that I had ever heard . . . Dylan was a revolutionary. Bob freed your mind the way Elvis freed your body. He showed us that just because the music was innately physical didn't mean it was anti-intellectual. He had the vision and the talent to make a pop song that contained the whole world. He invented a new way a pop singer could sound, broke through the limitations of what a recording artist could achieve and changed the face of rock and roll forever . . . To this day, wherever great rock music is being made, there is the shadow of Bob Dylan . . . So

In January 1988, Dylan was inducted into the Rock and Roll Hall of Fame by Bruce Springsteen, who paid him a graceful and eloquent tribute. Dylan contributed 'Like a Rolling Stone' and 'All Along the Watchtower' – the latter in a duet with George Harrison – to the celebrations at the Waldorf-Astoria in New York.

© 1988 Ron Delany/LGI/Rex Features

The original Traveling Wilburys:
Nelson (George Harrison), Lefty
(Roy Orbison), Lucky (Dylan), Otis
(Jeff Lynne) and Charlie (Tom Petty).

I'm just here tonight to say thanks, to say I wouldn't be here without you, to say that there isn't a soul in this room who doesn't owe you his thanks, and to steal a line from one of your songs — whether you like it or not, "You was the brother that I never had."' Springsteen was inducting a visibly moved Dylan into the Rock and Roll Hall of Fame, alongside the idols, dead and alive, who had inspired him over the radio waves thirty and more years earlier.

One day in April, another

Hall of Famer, George Harrison, called to ask if he could record a track in Dylan's Malibu garage. He didn't actually have a song written, but he brought along a friend, Jeff Lynne, the leader of ELO, to help out — and, since Lynne was in Los Angeles to produce the great veteran Roy Orbison, that soon made four. Harrison called up Tom Petty to ask if he'd return a borrowed guitar, and that made five: the Traveling Wilburys were born. When their album came out before Christmas, with fake identities for the participants

(Dylan was 'Lucky Wilbury'), it was like a tour-bus running gag that had been turned into a neat bit of late-eighties marketing, but it had some good moments. Despite Lynne's freeze-dried production, Dylan's 'Tweeter and the Monkey Man' was a perfect piece of surrealistic storytelling, done in two takes. A tour through a theme park called rock and roll, *The Traveling Wilburys Vol 1* yielded hit singles and became Dylan's only double-platinum album to date. Sadly, only a few weeks after its release, Roy Orbison — his career taking off after many years on the oldies circuit — died of a heart attack at his home in Tennessee.

Before the Wilburys climbed the charts, Dylan had released another in his lengthening series of dud albums. *Down in the Groove* seemed to have been assembled from more cutting-room floor sweepings. Who really needed Dylan's lacklustre version of Wilbert Harrison's old R&B standard 'Let's Stick Together'? At the end, though, long after most people would have given up, came a trilogy of serious pieces. In 'Ninety Miles an Hour Down a Dead-End Street' he took a country song about adultery, removed the tempo, added a male gospel quartet, and came up with a brilliant example of the sort of idiomatic cross-matching for which Ry Cooder had become famous. A skipping version of 'Shenandoah', all mandolin and piping harmonica, had a Huck Finn-ish charm. Finally, 'Rank Stranger' created the atmosphere of a strange, alien, backwoods America, Dylan's straining voice answered by an arching, echoing bass, as if it were coming from the depths of a dream.

For a decade, since his divorce, Dylan had been linked with a number of women: principally the singers Helena Springs and Clydie King, the actress Sally Kirkland, and Carol Childs – an A&R executive with David Geffen's Hollywood-based record company. Yet strangely, the author of 'Don't Think Twice' and 'She Belongs to Me' hadn't written a decent love song since *Blood on the Tracks.*

From the outside, Dylan's life appeared to be uncentred, unfocused, its domestic passages divided between the mansion in Malibu and the farm outside Minneapolis, but its true development was increasingly played out on the concert stage – particularly since his forays into the recording studio had less and less relevance to any sort of artistic evolution.

Around this time, Dylan said an extraordinary thing: 'I can't figure out sometimes if people think I'm alive or

dead.' Flip and cynical as it may have been, that remark nevertheless suggested the sort of pressure that might unhinge a man. But he also remarked that he couldn't complain, really: 'I *did* it, you know? I did what I wanted to do. And I'm still doing it.' Now he seemed to be finding solace in activity, however meaningless.

The road – which had almost killed him twenty years earlier – turned out to be the best answer to the problems he was facing: he discovered that it was where he could both be Bob Dylan and escape from himself. The road was hotel rooms, limousines, airports, dark glasses, one-sided duels with journalists: a familiar disguise. There may no longer have been a real agenda to his work, but on stage he could take all the Bob Dylans he'd ever been and mould them into any form he felt like inhabiting. In Paris one night in the eighties, he sang for two hours in every voice he'd ever used, switching back and forth just for the hell of it. One of his lines came to life: 'And I remember every face/Of every man who put me here . . .'

He no longer sold even the moderate volume of records that he'd managed during his heyday (even then he had never achieved anything approaching the sales of Presley or the Beatles), but his notoriety seemed

undiminished; his cult extended from young girls who showed up at his front door on his birthday to the gaggles of greying academics who organized Dylan seminars. He was now surrounded by minders and bodyguards, cutting him off from contact with his friends as well as his audience – although no hired hands were more effective than his own uncommunicative nature, which caused him both to attend his own rehearsals without speaking, and to shy away from any sort of random contact with fans.

By the late eighties, this life was clearly taking a toll. His weight seemed to fluctuate, his face was sometimes jowly – he didn't have the appearance of a man who was taking care of himself. He looked vulnerable, and sometimes a bit lost. He'd always said that he didn't have any answers; now, for the first time, it was possible to think that he might be telling the truth. Some nights, as he fled from himself like a man in a hall of mirrors, you had to peer very hard to see the outline of the boy from the cover of *Freewheelin'.*

Then, suddenly, for no apparent reason, everything came back into focus. In March 1989, Dylan went down to New Orleans to start working on a new album with Daniel Lanois, U2's producer, whom he'd met while contributing a little singing and harmonica to their album *Rattle and Hum*. Lanois, who favoured the use of minimum technology and unorthodox surroundings to break the plush sameness of conventional recording studios, found an old apartment building and imported the equipment to turn it into a temporary location for the making of *Oh Mercy*.

In his work with U2, Robbie Robertson, the Neville Brothers and Peter Gabriel, Lanois had shown a fondness for natural sounds and a gift for layering sound with an unusual depth of focus, using slender means to create a cinematic effect without overloading the frame. In particular, his exquisite version of 'With God on Our Side' with the Nevilles had shown both imagination and sensitivity to a difficult song. Under Lanois's ministrations, Dylan didn't have to strive to sound relaxed, as he had since the late seventies: his singing was unforced, accurate and expressive, and somehow Lanois coaxed from him a set of entirely satisfactory songs. 'Everything Is Broken', a simple blues shuffle set against a heavily reverberating guitar riff reminiscent of the Staple Singers' old records, became a 'Subterranean Homesick Blues' for fretful fortysomethings: 'Broken bodies/Broken

bones/Broken voices/On broken phones . . .' It could never have sounded so taut, so wrinkle-free, without Lanois's ability to focus the sound while keeping its spontaneity. 'Man in the Long Black Coat' was the other favourite, a western ballad harking back to the mood of *Pat Garrett and Billy the Kid*. But the whole album was confident, coherent, able to compete on level terms with young pretenders like REM and the Cowboy Junkies. Around the world, critics reached for a single phrase: his best since *Blood on the Tracks*.

In May, six months before the album's release, Dylan flew to Sweden to begin what became known as the Never-Ending Tour, featuring a three-piece band: G.E. Smith, an extrovert guitar-slinger roped in from Hall & Oates, bassist Kenny Aaronson, and Christopher Parker on drums. As usual, the sets were played off the cuff, but even the early shows had an astonishing impact. The levels were turned right up, the guitars sliced the air and the drums bounced off the walls. Dylan set his mouth into a death's-head grin and raced through his whole history, from a bent-out-of-shape 'Barbara Allen' to a fast 'Like a Rolling Stone' that was sung entirely on one note and yet somehow managed to be a dazzling masterpiece of vocal

phrasing. Synchronization wasn't there, but this was nevertheless maximum rock and roll that, with magnificent perversity, contradicted the mellow pacing and reflective mood of *Oh Mercy*.

The tour went to America and wound on for the rest of the year. In January 1990, though, Dylan took a big step back. Instead of persuading Lanois to record a follow-up, he moved on to another hot young producer: Don Was, half of the avant-garde soul revue Was (Not Was). Perhaps it was the influence of being back in Los Angeles; whatever the cause, *Under the Red Sky* was an instant return to the bad old days of content-free songs and flailing attempts to sound like various familiar kinds of Bob Dylan. The low-point came in the first track, a song called 'Wiggle Wiggle' which was less an amusing novelty than an insult to his listeners. The track was graced by the presence of Slash, the lead guitarist with the LA rockers Guns N' Roses; reportedly, Dylan invited him to play 'exactly like Django Reinhardt'.

While the album was in preparation, he and the touring band returned to the road – with a five-hour, forty-song familiarization session in front of the audience at Toad's Place in New Haven,

THE HOODED MAN AT THE RDS ARENA IN DUBLIN ON 3 JUNE 1989, ONE YEAR INTO THE NEVER-ENDING TOUR. HIS ENCORES INCLUDED 'EILEEN AROON', LEARNT MANY YEARS EARLIER FROM THE CLANCY BROTHERS AND TOMMY MAKEM.

Connecticut on 12 January. A couple of weeks later they were back in Europe, where they played four nights at the Grand Rex Theatre in Paris and six at the Hammersmith Odeon in London, delighting fans whose wildest dreams had not incorporated a return to medium-sized venues where the sound could be controlled properly and a decent rapport established across the footlights. Now the music was better organized, the mood gentler and the acoustic sequence – in which Dylan and Smith created some fine guitar interplay – particularly impressive. In Paris, Dylan appeared to enjoy the ceremony at which he was made a Commander of the Order of Arts and Letters by the French culture minister, Jack Lang.

Back in the USA, Dylan played at a tribute to Orbison with the Byrds and recorded the Wilburys' second album – titled *Volume 3* – before hitting the road even harder for the remainder of the year, while the release of *Under the Red Sky* brought the familiar sound of gnashing teeth. 'Obviously, I'm not going to be around for ever,' he once observed. 'The day is going to come when there aren't going to be any more records and then people won't be able to say, well, this one's not as good as the last one.'

At the Grammy Awards ceremony on 20 February 1991, Dylan received a 'lifetime achievement' award. Mick Jagger acted as his cheerleader as Dylan and his band performed 'Masters of War' to a Radio City Music Hall audience that had the Gulf conflict on its mind.

A VIDEO SHOOT IN NEW YORK, 1991.
DESPITE HIS INTEREST IN FILM, AND
ALTHOUGH THE FIRST TWO MINUTES OF
DON'T LOOK BACK IN 1965 MAY HAVE
CONSTITUTED THE FIRST ROCK VIDEO,
DYLAN COULD MAKE NOTHING OF THE
FORM IN ITS MTV INCARNATION.

Now Dylan was going to be fifty. At the Grammy Awards ceremony in January 1991, he was given a lifetime achievement award. Columbia prepared to release a three-CD set called *The Bootleg Series*, making such important features of the Dylan output as 'Mama You Been on My Mind', 'Farewell Angelina', 'Blind Willie McTell' and 'Series of Dreams' officially available for the first time. An English newspaper prepared a feature in which fifty people said what they'd give him for his birthday in May. 'Anonymity,' said Dave Van Ronk and Bobby Neuwirth, independently. 'Something to believe in,' said Billy Bragg. 'A brand-new leopard-skin pill-box hat,' said Marianne Faithfull, who'd worn the original in 1965. 'Peace of mind,' said Johnny Cash. 'Fifty dimes and fifty tambourines,' said Roger McGuinn. 'My Cadillac,' said John Lee Hooker. 'A pair of sneakers,' said Judy Collins. 'A good time,' said Dana

REHEARSING FOR THE GUITAR LEGENDS FESTIVAL IN SEVILLE IN THE SUMMER OF 1991. DYLAN PLAYED 'ALL ALONG THE WATCHTOWER' WITH A BAND INCLUDING RICHARD THOMPSON AND JACK BRUCE, SANG 'BOOTS OF SPANISH LEATHER', THE RY COODER/JOHN HIATT 'ACROSS THE BORDERLINE' AND THE OLD POP STANDARD 'ANSWER ME' WITH THOMPSON, AND JAMMED WITH KEITH RICHARDS ON A HILARIOUS 'SHAKE, RATTLE AND ROLL'.

REX FEATURES

Even at this stage, England was still giving him trouble. Here, in February 1991, he ducks out of Heathrow, dodging the paparazzi.

Opposite: A rock and roller at fifty; Milan, 8 June 1991

Gillespie, who'd shared some of the 1965 British tour with him. 'A ball of wax and the whole nine yards,' said Leonard Cohen. 'A new hat and a good song,' said Mick Jagger. 'That polka-dot shirt he wore in 1965,' said Bob Geldof. 'Youth and beauty and no more biographies,' said Suze Rotolo.

On a freezing night that January, the traffic locked solid on the snowbound London streets, we shuffled back to Hammersmith Odeon to see the latest episode of the saga. Backed by an anonymous new four-piece band, Dylan came on wearing a strange boxy plaid jacket that looked as though it belonged to someone else, and performed with a sort of wilful lethargy, constantly picking up the wrong harmonicas, forgetting words, leaving out entire verses of 'Desolation Row' and in general behaving like the boy whose ambition upon graduation from high school was to join Little Richard.

As he mangled some old favourite, reducing a fine melody and an incomparable lyric to an indecipherable racket, I turned to the occupant of the next seat. 'Well,' I said, 'I suppose they're his songs, and he can do what he likes with them.' 'Yes,' she replied, and thought it over for a few seconds. 'That seems to be his idea, too.'

BIBLIOGRAPHY

This account was compiled with the help of the following publications:

John Bauldie, booklet accompanying *The Bootleg Series* (Columbia Records, 1991)

Jonathan Cott, *Dylan* (Vermilion, 1984)

Cameron Crowe, booklet accompanying *Biograph* (Columbia Records, 1985)

Bob Dylan, *Tarantula* (MacGibbon & Kee, 1971); *Writings and Drawings* (Jonathan Cape, 1973); *Lyrics 1962–1985* (Jonathan Cape, 1987)

Jonathon Green, *Days in the Life* (Heinemann, 1988)

Michael Gross, *Bob Dylan: An Illustrated History* (Elm Tree, 1978)

John Hammond, *John Hammond on Record* (Ridge Press/Summit Books, 1977; Penguin, 1978)

Clinton Heylin, *Behind the Shades* (Viking, 1991)

Patrick Humphries and John Bauldie, *Oh No! Not Another Bob Dylan Book* (Square One, 1991)

Daniel Kramer, *Bob Dylan* (Castle Books, 1967; Plexus, 1991)

Michael Krogsgaard, *Positively Bob Dylan: A Thirty-Year Discography, Concert & Recording Session Guide, 1960–1991* (Popular Culture, Ink/Scandinavian Institute for Rock Research, 1991)

Craig McGregor (Ed.), *Bob Dylan: A Retrospective* (William Morrow, 1972)

Anthony Scaduto, *Bob Dylan: An Intimate Biography* (W.H. Allen, 1971)

Robert Shelton, *No Direction Home* (New English Library, 1986)

Sam Shepard, *Rolling Thunder Logbook* (Penguin, 1978)

Bob Spitz, *Dylan: A Biography* (McGraw-Hill, 1988)

Jean Stein, *Edie* (Jonathan Cape, 1982)

Elizabeth Thompson and David Gutman (Eds), *The Dylan Companion* (Macmillan, 1990)

Interviews by Jonathan Cott, Robert Palmer, Kurt Loder and others

With thanks to Howard Thompson

INDEX